MARY

— All in One —

MARY

— All in One —

My Favourite ***One Pan, One Pot, One Dish*** Recipes

BBC
BOOKS

Contents

Introduction

This is a collection of my favourite one pot, one pan and one dish recipes from across the years. All the recipes we've chosen are ones we really enjoy and cook often at home; they are also the ones readers cook the most and we have been told are the most popular. It's so easy when it's just one dish to cook, serve and wash up! We're all looking to make life a bit easier, and a one pot dish is a great way to start. Dishes such as our Chicken Tartiflette (see page 70) with potatoes, chicken and the sauce all in one tray are a crowd pleaser and can be taken straight to the table to serve. Whether you're cooking for a midweek supper, lunch with friends, making a dish for a picnic or you're taking something round to a friend in need, you'll find a wonderful variety of recipes here. From one pot casseroles like Tuscan Chicken (see page 87), Cottage Pie with Crushed Potato Topping (see page 123) and Orzo with Broad Beans, Peas, Lemon and Thyme (see page 140), to one tray roasts like Mediterranean All-in-one Chicken (see page 82), French Slow-roast Lamb with Rataouille (see page 135) and One Tray Sausage Supper (see page 115), there is something for everyone.

We've included dishes that can be made ahead and freezer instructions where appropriate, so you'll have something at the ready if people turn up at short notice. All my life, whenever we go on holiday for a rented stay, I take a cooked all-in-one dish for the first night. You'll find lots of great ideas here that could be put in the boot of the car, and others that can be stored at home in the freezer and served to unexpected visitors.

Moules Marinière (see page 45) an easy, last-minute, one pan supper and so quick, too. We always like to include a classic fish pie and here we've shared our ultimate recipe – Glorious Fish Pie (see page 48)! The Salmon and Fennel One Pot Wonder (see page 59) is simple and so very good, and all children love Hobie's Tuna Pasta Bake (see page 61); it is inexpensive to make but delicious. Another good value one pot is the vegetarian Humble Pie (see page 160) – filled with different vegetables and topped with puff pastry, it is really inexpensive and quick to make, and filling, too.

Some dishes might benefit from pasta or rice served alongside, or a green salad or tenderstem broccoli to brighten the plate, but all the hard work is done in one dish on the hob or in the oven. We haven't included first courses, as we would usually, but share our favourite soups and dips, which would work as a first course but are also good as a light lunch. The Ten-minute Tomato Soup (see page 25) is so simple – when the weather is cold, you can make it from ingredients you'd usually have in the cupboard – while soups such as the Smoked Haddock Chowder (see page 27) and Chicken Noodle Laksa (see page 28) are filling enough for supper.

There are glorious salads for a summer lunch, but which would also package up in reusable plastic or bamboo containers for a picnic. Recipes like our Avocado Caesar Salad (see page 174) – just take the dressing in a jam jar to pour over before you eat – and the Hot-smoked Salmon Rice and Asparagus Salad (see page 184) would be so much nicer to take to eat for lunch at work or for a picnic than sandwiches. The Cheese and Garlic Tear-and-share Scones (see page 234) are wonderful straight from the oven, though they freeze well and are quick to reheat.

When it comes to baking, the all-in-one method is the best. Make sure to use baking spread straight from the fridge and don't overbeat or overbake the cakes or they will be dry. I always have a Chocolate Fudge Cake (see page 220) in the freezer, well wrapped, for emergency visitors. It is delicious and everyone always asks for the recipe. The Chocolate Steamed Pudding (see page 242) may seem a bit old-fashioned but it is just so good and there's plenty of sauce to go alongside, which is how I like it. The Pear and Blueberry Galette (see page 251) is pretty and so simple, and it elevates a basic pudding into something special. Our Quickest-ever Lemon Meringue Pie (see page 268) is best eaten on the day it is made, and is so quick.

Whether a recipe is made all in one pan when you're frying, all in one dish when you cook in the oven, all in one tray when you roast or bake, or the ingredients are mixed all in one bowl when you bake, these one pot recipes will become your favourites, too.

Mary Berry

Cook's Notes

I always like to include some general tips to help make your cooking at home as simple and straightforward as possible. I want everyone to enjoy preparing their meals, as well as the process of sharing them with friends and family.

Read the recipe

Make sure to read the recipe all the way through to the end before starting to cook. You can check you have all the correct equipment, that the oven is set to the right temperature and that all the ingredients are weighed accurately before you start. It is so important, particularly with baking.

Metric and imperial

I have provided both metric and imperial measurements. It's best to stick to one or the other when you are following a recipe – particularly if you are baking.

Oven and grill temperatures

As ovens and grills vary in the amount of heat they produce, you may need to cook a dish for slightly longer or shorter than the recipe states. You will get to know your oven in time, but it can be helpful to use an oven thermometer.

Ovenproof frying pans and flameproof casseroles

A number of my recipes for savoury stews and one pan dishes begin on the hob and end up in the oven. I tend to use wide-based, deep frying pans that have a lid, as the ones I have at home are ovenproof, but it would be just as good to use a flameproof casserole. So long as it has a lid that fits and is suitable to use on the hob and in the oven, it will do the job.

Tins and dishes

Always use the correct size of tins and dishes, otherwise the food can cook differently. If your roasting or cake tin is slightly larger than I recommend, the liquid may evaporate more quickly and the sauce may dry out, or the sponge may be thin and overbake. Conversely, if your tin is smaller, the sauce may be too runny or the cake undercooked. This is even more important when you are cooking an all-in-one dish – if the sauce isn't right, there isn't something else coming out of the oven or off the hob with which to hide the error!

You'll also find pies and casseroles cook more quickly in an enamel tin than in a cast-iron dish – the materials heat up at different rates and so the heat is transferred to the food more quickly in some dishes than others.

Scales and measuring spoons

I find digital scales really are the best and the most accurate. Another essential kitchen item is a set of measuring spoons for measuring baking powder, spices and small amounts of liquids. All spoon measurements in this book are level, unless otherwise stated.

Handheld whisks and blenders

These hand mixers are so useful for a number of different recipes. They are more affordable than the designer free-standing mixers and do just as good a job. The hand whisks are smaller than with a large mixer, so it may take a little longer to thicken if you are using one.

Vegetarian and vegan recipes

More and more often, I will choose to cook without meat at home. I have included a wide variety of vegetarian dishes and they are some of my favourite recipes in the book. There are a handful of vegan recipes, too, and other vegetarian dishes that can be adapted to be vegan.

Free-range meat

Buy the best-quality meat you can afford. British farmers have some of the highest food standards in the world and it really does make a difference. Animals should be looked after and loved, fed properly and regularly, and respected for the nourishment they provide. I always use free-range chicken and eggs.

Sustainable fish

Buy fish that is sustainably sourced. It will advertise itself as such on the packet, or ask at the fish counter in your local supermarket or fishmonger. The levels of fish stocks do change, though, so while I have tried to ensure all the recipes include fish that are on the sustainability list, do swap one for another, if necessary.

Eggs

Use large, free-range eggs, unless otherwise stated.

Soups and Dips

Celeriac and Watercress Soup

Vegetable Miso Soup

Carrot, Sweet Potato and Ginger Soup

Ten-minute Tomato Soup

Smoked Haddock Chowder

Chicken Noodle Laksa

Artichoke Dip

Sardine Paté

Soured Cream and Herb Dip

Guacamole with Tomato and Chilli

Party Ploughman's

Celeriac and Watercress Soup

I am a soup addict, and it is my lunchtime staple all year round. With this lovely soup, avoid keeping it hot on the hob as the watercress will lose its vibrant green colour. If it's a little on the thick side, add more stock. The celeriac makes it a bit more substantial and filling.

Serves 6

2 tbsp sunflower oil
2 large onions, roughly chopped
750g (1lb 10oz) peeled celeriac, diced (prepared weight)
1.5 litres (2½ pints) vegetable or chicken stock
100g (3½oz) watercress
About 4 tbsp full-fat crème fraîche or pouring double cream

1. Heat the oil in a large, deep saucepan over a medium heat. Add the onions and fry for 5 minutes until just starting to brown. Add the celeriac and fry for 4–5 minutes, stirring occasionally, until starting to colour. Pour in the stock and season with salt and pepper.
2. Cover with a lid and bring to the boil. Reduce the heat and simmer for 15–20 minutes until completely tender.
3. Add most of the watercress, reserving a few sprigs to garnish, and stir over the heat for 2–3 minutes until wilted.
4. Blend the soup until smooth, either with a hand blender or in a free-standing blender or food processor (see tip).
5. Swirl through the crème fraîche or double cream and check the seasoning. Serve piping hot with the reserved watercress sprigs.

MARY'S TIPS

If you have any leftover celeriac, add it to mash. If using a free-standing blender or food processor, reheat the soup before serving, as it will cool down in the machine.

Freezes well after step 4. Defrost, reheat and add the crème fraîche or double cream to serve.

Vegetable Miso Soup

A stock-based Japanese soup, quick and fresh. My version is made using vegetables, but you could add chicken or tofu. If you like a little heat, add a sprinkle of dried chilli flakes before serving. Shiitake mushrooms add a lovely depth of flavour; if you can't find them fresh, use dried, but you'll need to soak them first. Savoy cabbage has a wonderful flavour and texture, though you could use pointed spring cabbage instead.

Serves 4–6

4 tbsp white miso paste
1.4 litres (2½ pints) vegetable or chicken stock
2 tsp grated fresh root ginger
1 bunch of spring onions (about 6–8), thinly sliced
2 tbsp soy sauce
1 tbsp light muscovado sugar
200g (7oz) shiitake mushrooms, sliced
½ small savoy cabbage, shredded (see introduction)

To serve

½ bunch of coriander, leaves roughly chopped
1–2 tsp toasted sesame oil

1. Measure the miso paste into a bowl. Gradually add 150ml (¼ pint) of the chicken stock and whisk together until smooth.
2. Pour the remaining stock into a large saucepan and place over a high heat. Add the miso mixture and whisk until smooth, then tip in the grated ginger and bring to the boil. Add the spring onions, soy sauce, sugar, mushrooms and cabbage, then simmer for 5–10 minutes, until the vegetables are tender.
3. Season to taste with salt and pepper. Spoon the soup into bowls, sprinkle over the chopped coriander leaves and a few drops of the toasted sesame oil. Serve hot.

MARY'S TIPS

This soup can be made a day ahead and kept in the fridge. It will separate and the miso will become cloudy, but give it a good stir and reheat gently before adding the coriander leaves and sesame oil to serve.

Not suitable for freezing.

Carrot, Sweet Potato and Ginger Soup

Warming and full of goodness, the ginger gives a natural kick and a refreshing flavour to this soup. It is also very soothing for the digestive system, so I'm told.

Serves 4–6

2 tbsp sunflower oil
2 onions, roughly chopped
500g (1lb 2oz) carrots, roughly sliced
500g (1lb 2oz) sweet potatoes, peeled and roughly chopped
25g (1oz) fresh root ginger, peeled and grated, plus a little extra for garnish
1.5 litres (2½ pints) chicken or vegetable stock

1. Place the oil in a deep saucepan over a high heat. Add the onions and fry for a few minutes. Add the carrots, sweet potatoes and ginger and fry for 3–4 minutes.
2. Pour in the stock, cover with a lid and bring up to the boil. Reduce the heat and simmer for about 15–20 minutes until the vegetables are tender.
3. Remove from the heat and season with salt and black pepper. Blend with a hand blender or whiz in a food processor until smooth.
4. Check the seasoning, sprinkle over some extra grated ginger and serve piping hot with your favourite bread.

MARY'S TIPS

The soup can be made up to 2 days ahead and kept in the fridge. Reheat gently to serve.

Freezes well.

Ten-minute Tomato Soup

A homemade recipe to rival the nostalgic comfort of classic tinned cream of tomato. The pesto adds a lovely flavour, but it is still very good without it. With no onions to chop or tomatoes to skin, this soup is quick, easy and delicious. In fact, it is one of my favourite family soups, as I always have the ingredients in the cupboard.

Serves 6

- 6 sun-dried tomatoes in oil, roughly chopped
- 2 garlic cloves, finely grated
- 3 × 400g tins chopped tomatoes
- 500ml (18fl oz) chicken or vegetable stock
- 2 tsp caster sugar
- 150ml (¼ pint) milk
- 150ml (¼ pint) double cream
- 3–4 tsp fresh basil pesto (see introduction)

1. Set a large, deep pan over a medium heat and add 1 tablespoon of oil from the sun-dried tomatoes. Add the garlic and stir-fry for a few seconds.
2. Tip in the sun-dried and tinned tomatoes, add the stock and sugar (see tip) and bring to the boil, stirring all the while. Season with salt and pepper, then cover with a lid, reduce the heat and simmer for 10 minutes.
3. Remove from the heat and, using a hand blender, blitz the soup in the pan, or purée in a food processor. Stir in the milk and cream and check the seasoning before heating through on the hob.
4. Serve hot with ½ teaspoon of basil pesto swirled on top of each bowl of soup.

MARY'S TIPS

The sugar brings out the flavour of the tomatoes and helps balance their acidity.

Can be made up to 3 days ahead. Freezes well without the milk and cream. Defrost and reheat until piping hot, then stir them in before serving.

Smoked Haddock Chowder

A good substantial soup – a meal in itself served with lots of crusty bread. I have used full-fat milk to give a good creamy flavour. If you only have a low-fat milk, just add a little cream before serving.

Serves 6

55g (2oz) butter
4 large shallots, chopped
6 celery sticks, sliced
2 medium carrots, chopped into 1cm (½in) dice
200g (7oz) button mushrooms, sliced
450g (1lb) old potatoes, peeled and cut into 2cm (¾in) chunks
40g (1½oz) plain flour
600ml (1 pint) fish or vegetable stock
600ml (1 pint) full-fat milk
30g (1oz) petits pois
700g (1lb 9oz) smoked haddock fillets, skinned and chopped into bite-sized pieces
100g (3½oz) baby spinach
Freshly chopped dill, to garnish

1. Heat the butter in a large saucepan over a medium heat. Add the shallots, celery and carrots, and stir to coat in the butter. Cover with a lid and cook gently over a low heat for about 3 minutes until beginning to soften. Add the mushrooms and potatoes, and cook for a further 1–2 minutes.

2. Stir in the flour, then add the stock and milk, pouring it in gradually and stirring until smooth. Season with pepper to taste, adding no salt at this stage as the fish can be very salty. Bring the mixture to the boil and simmer for 10–15 minutes, or until the vegetables are tender.

3. Add the peas and the smoked haddock to the vegetable mixture and simmer gently for a couple of minutes until the fish is cooked.

4. Adjust the seasoning to taste, stir in the spinach and garnish with dill to serve.

MARY'S TIPS

Be gentle with the chowder – no fast boiling or rapid mixing; you want all the flavours to infuse but without breaking up the fish and potatoes.

Can be made up to 1 day ahead and stored in the fridge overnight. Not suitable for freezing.

Chicken Noodle Laksa

Laksa is a popular spicy noodle soup in Peranakan cooking – a combination of Chinese and Malay cuisine found in Malaysia, Singapore and Indonesia. Lucinda, who has been testing recipes with us for many years, inspired this wonderfully warming soup.

Serves 4

- 2 skinless and boneless chicken breasts, sliced into thin strips
- 3 tbsp sunflower oil
- 115g (4oz) rice noodles
- 6 spring onions, finely sliced
- 2 × 400g tins coconut milk
- 2 tsp fish sauce
- 1 stick of lemongrass, bashed
- Juice of ½ lime
- Coriander leaves, to serve (optional)

For the spicy paste

- 6 spring onions, roughly sliced
- 1 red chilli, deseeded and chopped
- 4cm (1½in) piece of fresh root ginger, peeled and grated
- 2 garlic cloves, finely grated
- 3 tbsp smooth peanut butter
- 2 tsp fresh lime juice
- 1 tbsp light muscovado sugar

1. First make the spicy paste. Place all the ingredients in a food processor and whiz until finely chopped, or grind with a pestle and mortar.
2. Spoon 2 tablespoons of the spicy paste into a bowl. Add the chicken strips, season with salt and pepper, and toss to coat.
3. Heat a large, deep frying pan or wok over a high heat. Add 2 tablespoons of the sunflower oil and, when hot, tip in the chicken strips and fry for about 3 minutes, until golden all over and just cooked through. Remove with a slotted spoon and set aside.
4. Place the rice noodles in a shallow dish and pour over enough hot water to cover. Leave for 10–15 minutes or until the noodles have softened. Drain and refresh the noodles under cold water, then snip them into short lengths and set aside.
5. Meanwhile, heat the remaining oil in the pan or wok (no need to wash it first), add the spring onions and the remaining spicy paste and fry for 1 minute. Stir in the coconut milk, fish sauce and lemongrass. Bring to the boil, then reduce the heat and simmer for about 5 minutes.
6. Add the chicken to the soup and simmer for 3–4 minutes. Divide the noodles between four warmed bowls. Remove the lemongrass from the soup and add the lime juice. Ladle the soup over the noodles and sprinkle with coriander to serve.

MARY'S TIPS

Placing the noodles in the bowls first ensures everyone has the same amount.

The chicken mixture can be made up to 8 hours ahead and the noodles soaked just before serving.

Artichoke Dip

This is so delicious and quick to make that it will become a real favourite. It's great for entertaining – serve with toasted sourdough, tortilla crisps or crudités. Once you start eating, you'll find it hard to stop! Artichoke hearts preserved in oil would do just as well here. Whether from a tin or a jar, they need to be well drained; if they are too wet, they will make the dip runny and watery. After draining the artichokes, empty them into a bowl and give each one an extra squeeze to release the liquid inside.

Serves 6

- 200g (7oz) low-fat mayonnaise
- 150g (5oz) soured cream
- 115g (4oz) mature Cheddar, finely grated
- 25g (1oz) Parmesan, finely grated
- ¼ small onion, roughly chopped
- 1 garlic clove, grated
- 1 × 400g tin artichoke hearts (see introduction), drained
- Snipped chives, to garnish

1. Measure the mayonnaise and soured cream into a food processor, then add the two cheeses, the onion, garlic and artichokes. Season with salt and freshly ground black pepper and whiz until blended.

2. Check the seasoning, then spoon into a bowl. Sprinkle with a few snipped chives to serve.

MARY'S TIPS

Can be made up to 2 days ahead and kept in the fridge, but bear in mind that the garlic flavour will get stronger the longer it infuses.

Not suitable for freezing.

Sardine Paté

Perfect for a quick lunch – so easy to make and using storecupboard ingredients. If you don't have any dill, parsley would also be nice.

Serves 4

84g sardine fillets in olive oil, drained and bones removed (drained weight)

55g (2oz) butter, softened

125g (4½oz) full-fat cream cheese

2 tbsp freshly chopped dill, plus a few small sprigs, to garnish

1 tsp tomato purée

1 tsp fresh lemon juice, to taste

Lemon wedges, to serve

1. Tip the sardine fillets into small food processor with the butter, cream cheese, dill and tomato purée. Season well with salt and freshly ground black pepper and blend quickly to a rough texture. Add some lemon juice and mix well. Taste and adjust the lemon.
2. Spoon into four small ramekins, cover with clingfilm and chill in the fridge for 2 hours.
3. Serve on toasted bread with lemon wedges alongside and garnished with a sprig of dill.

MARY'S TIPS

We like to make this with sardine fillets, but you could use other tinned fish, if preferred.

The paté will keep in the fridge for up to 4 days.

Not suitable for freezing.

Party Dips

These dips really complement each other and are great for a party to serve with bread sticks, tortillas, crisps or vegetable crudités.

Soured Cream and Herb Dip

Serves 4–6

- 300ml (½ pint) soured cream
- 1 × 165g tub full-fat cream cheese
- 2 tbsp very finely chopped parsley
- 2 tbsp very finely chopped mint
- 2 tbsp very finely chopped basil
- 1 garlic clove, finely grated
- 1 tbsp fresh lemon juice

1. Measure everything into a bowl, season well with salt and pepper, and mix to combine.
2. Cover with clingfilm and chill in the fridge for a minimum of 2 hours for the flavours to combine and develop. The longer you leave the dip, the stronger it will taste.

MARY'S TIPS

The dip can be kept, covered, in the fridge for up to 3 days. Not suitable for freezing.

Guacamole with Tomato and Chilli

Serves 4–6

- 2 ripe avocados, peeled and destoned
- 4 large spring onions, finely chopped
- 1 large tomato, quartered, deseeded and finely chopped
- 1 small green chilli, deseeded and finely chopped
- Juice of ½–1 lime
- 1 garlic clove, finely grated
- Small bunch of coriander, leaves finely chopped

1. Roughly mash the avocado in a bowl with a fork. Add all the remaining ingredients, mix well and season with lots of salt and pepper.
2. Cover with clingfilm and chill in the fridge for at least 30 minutes for the flavours to develop.

MARY'S TIPS

The dip can be made up to 4 hours ahead. It will keep for a day in the fridge, but will discolour if left too long. Not suitable for freezing.

Party Ploughman's

Great to serve as a sharing platter at a large party, this is all about choosing the very best ingredients (see tip) and presenting them in an attractive way.

Serves 6–8

1 cucumber
2 large Romano peppers, quartered lengthways and deseeded
Olive oil, for drizzling
2 tbsp balsamic glaze
350g (12oz) asparagus spears, trimmed
3 tbsp sour cream
1 tbsp white wine vinegar
200g (7oz) large green olives in oil
150g (5oz) smoked salmon slices
1 small head of celery, sliced into batons
6 slices Parma ham
200g (7oz) Cheddar, sliced into wedges
150g (5oz) Boursin cheese
200g (7oz) cherry tomatoes, halved
100g (3½oz) mini mozzarella balls
1 olive ciabatta loaf
Handful of fresh dill
1 lemon, cut into wedges

1. Preheat the oven to 220°C/Fan 200°C/Gas 7.
2. Slice the cucumber in half lengthways. Scoop out the seeds and slice thinly. Place in a colander, sprinkle with salt and leave for 1 hour. Rinse under cold water, then drain.
3. Place the peppers in a roasting tin and drizzle with olive oil. Roast in the oven for 20 minutes until tinged brown. Remove from the oven and drizzle with the balsamic glaze.
4. Blanch the asparagus in boiling salted water for 4 minutes. Drain and refresh under cold water, then drain again.
5. Measure the sour cream and white wine vinegar into a bowl. Add the sliced cucumber and season well with salt and freshly ground black pepper. Mix well, then spoon into a small dish or shallow bowl. Tip the olives into a separate small dish.
6. To assemble, arrange the smoked salmon at one end of a very large platter or board. Place the celery, roasted peppers, Parma ham, olives, asparagus, cucumber salad and sliced Cheddar around the board. Unwrap the Boursin and place in the centre.
7. Mix the tomatoes and mozzarella together in a small bowl and season, then spoon onto the platter.
8. Warm the bread, if liked, and cut into slices. Add the bread to the board and garnish with dill and lemon wedges to serve.

MARY'S TIPS

You do not have to be ruled by the cheese suggestions here. Choose ones that have different flavours and textures – perhaps a local soft cheese and a hard cheese with a more mature flavour.

Not suitable for freezing.

Fish and Shellfish

Prawn and Ginger Noodle Stir-fry

Moules Marinière

Roasting Tin Thai Salmon and Vegetables

Glorious Fish Pie

Cod and Spinach with Gremolata

Lemon Pepper Cod

Prawn and Salmon Herb Crumble

Haddock and Shrimp Feast

Salmon and Fennel One Pot Wonder

Hobie's Tuna Pasta Bake

Seafood Linguine with Fresh Tomato Sauce

Prawn and Ginger Noodle Stir-fry

Once all the ingredients are prepared, this can be cooked in no time, making it good to serve at the last minute. Present in individual bowls with some prawn crackers on the side.

Serves 4

150g (5oz) dried medium egg noodles
3 tbsp olive oil
2 large red peppers, deseeded and thinly sliced
1 red chilli, deseeded and finely chopped
8 spring onions, thinly sliced on the diagonal
115g (4oz) chestnut mushrooms, thickly sliced
3cm (1¼in) piece of fresh root ginger, peeled and grated
2 pak choi, thinly sliced, keeping white and green parts separate
350g (12oz) peeled raw king prawns

For the sauce

1 tbsp Chinese five-spice powder
3 tbsp soy sauce
3 tbsp runny honey
2 tsp white wine vinegar

To serve (optional)

4 pink radishes, thinly sliced
Juice of ½ lemon
2 tbsp freshly chopped coriander

1. Cook the noodles according to the packet instructions, drain and refresh in cold water. Mix the sauce ingredients together in a small bowl until smooth.
2. Heat the oil in a large, non-stick frying pan or wok over a high heat. Add the red peppers, chilli, spring onions, mushrooms, ginger and the white parts of the pak choi, and fry, stirring, for about 4 minutes, or until the vegetables are nearly cooked but still crisp.
3. Add the prawns and fry for a further minute, or until starting to turn pink.
4. Tip the drained noodles into the pan and add the green leaves of the pak choi, then fry for another minute or so, stirring to combine.
5. Pour the sauce over the mixture in the pan, stirring continuously. Season with salt and freshly ground black pepper. Once the prawns are completely pink, transfer to individual plates or bowls to serve immediately.
6. Garnish with the sliced radishes, squeeze over the lemon juice and scatter with the chopped coriander, if using.

MARY'S TIPS

The noodles can be cooked in advance and kept in the fridge, tossed with a little oil to stop them sticking. The vegetables can all be prepared ahead and stored in a freezer bag in the fridge.

Not suitable for freezing.

Moules Marinière

This is a classic and the ultimate sharing dish. Two big bowls of moules in the centre of the table, with crusty bread or fries – perfect. If any mussels are open before cooking, give them a tap. If they close, they are fine; if not, discard them. Likewise discard any that are still closed or broken after cooking.

Serves 2

2 tbsp olive oil
Knob of butter
4 large banana shallots, thinly sliced
4 garlic cloves, finely grated
1kg (2lb 4oz) ready-to-cook fresh mussels
150ml (¼ pint) white wine
150ml (¼ pint) pouring double cream
Juice of ½ lemon
Small bunch of parsley, leaves chopped

1. Heat the oil and butter in a wide-based, deep saucepan over a high heat. Add the shallots and fry for 3–4 minutes to soften. Add the garlic and fry for 10 seconds.
2. Tip the clean mussels into the pan and stir over the heat. Pour in the wine and bring up to the boil. Cover with a lid and boil for 3–4 minutes, giving the pan a shake every now and again, until the mussels have opened.
3. Remove the mussels with a slotted spoon and place in a dish.
4. Continue to boil the liquid until reduced by half (which should take around 5 minutes). Add the cream and boil for a few minutes. Taste and season well with salt and freshly ground black pepper.
5. Return the mussels to the pan, add the lemon juice and the parsley, and toss everything together. Serve at once while piping hot with crusty bread.

MARY'S TIPS

If you can't find 'ready-to-cook' mussels, place the fresh mussels in a large bowl of cold water and scrub to clean them. Remove any beards, which are the stringy threads on the side of the shell, and discard any broken mussels. Drain before cooking.

Make and serve immediately.

Not suitable for freezing.

Roasting Tin Thai Salmon and Vegetables

This dish has become a firm favourite of mine. And it's so easy to make, as the salmon, sauce and vegetables are all cooked together in one roasting tin in the oven. Thai basil is ideal here but if you don't have any, coriander works well too. Romano peppers are long and tapered with a sweet, fruity, mild flavour.

Serves 6

1 × 400ml (14fl oz) tin full-fat coconut milk

2 tbsp red Thai curry paste

1 fresh red chilli, deseeded and finely diced

1 large garlic clove, finely grated

6cm (2½in) piece of fresh root ginger, peeled and coarsely grated

Juice of 2 limes

2 tsp fish sauce

1 cauliflower, split into very small florets

2 Romano peppers, deseeded and cut into large pieces

3 banana shallots, halved

2 tbsp olive oil

1 tbsp runny honey

150g (5oz) baby courgettes, thinly sliced

6 thin salmon fillets (about 150g/5oz each), skinned

Freshly chopped Thai basil or coriander, to serve

1. Preheat the oven to 220°C/Fan 200°C/Gas 7.
2. Measure the coconut milk, Thai paste, chilli, garlic, ginger, lime juice and fish sauce into a small bowl and mix well.
3. Scatter the cauliflower florets, peppers and shallots into a large roasting tin or ovenproof dish. Add a tablespoon of the oil and mix well. Pour over half the sauce and drizzle over the honey. Roast in the oven for about 12–15 minutes until the vegetables are starting to brown.
4. Toss the courgettes in the remaining oil, season and add them to the tin. Nestle the salmon fillets in between the veg and spoon over the remaining sauce. Roast for a further 10 minutes until the salmon flesh is opaque pink and is just cooked.
5. Sprinkle over the Thai basil or coriander and serve.

MARY'S TIPS

Sauce can be made up to 8 hours ahead and the dish assembled when it's time to cook.

Not suitable for freezing.

Glorious Fish Pie

No book of one dish food would be complete without a comforting fish pie. This is one that all my family love.

Serves 6–8

- 100g (3½oz) butter
- 2 small leeks, thinly sliced
- 100g (3½oz) plain flour
- 900ml (1½ pints) hot milk
- 100g (3½oz) full-fat crème fraîche
- 2 tsp Dijon mustard
- Juice of ½ lemon
- Small bunch of dill, chopped
- 25g (1oz) Parmesan, grated
- 500g (1lb 2oz) fresh haddock, skinned and cut into chunks
- 500g (1lb 2oz) undyed smoked haddock, skinned and cut into chunks
- 4 eggs, hard-boiled, peeled and quartered

For the topping

- 1kg (2lb 4oz) potatoes, peeled and cut into even-sized cubes
- 2 tbsp milk
- 2 knobs of butter

1. You will need a 2.5 litre (4½ pint) ovenproof dish. Preheat the oven to 200°C/Fan 180°C/Gas 6.
2. Melt the butter in a deep, wide saucepan over a medium heat. Add the leeks and cook until softened. Stir in the flour and whisk over the heat for 1 minute. Blend in the hot milk, whisking until you have a smooth, thick sauce, then simmer for a few minutes.
3. Stir in the crème fraîche, mustard, lemon juice, dill and cheese, and season with salt and pepper. Remove the sauce from the heat and stir in the fish, then spoon everything into the ovenproof dish. Push the egg quarters into the mixture, so they are submerged in the sauce, then set aside to cool.
4. Meanwhile, put the potatoes in a large pan of cold salted water and bring to the boil. Boil for about 15 minutes until tender, then drain well and return to the pan. Add the milk and a knob of butter, season and mash well.
5. Spoon the mash on top of the fish, spreading it out, then run a fork over the surface to make a nice pattern. Dot the remaining butter on top of the pie.
6. Bake in the preheated oven for about 30–35 minutes until bubbling and golden on top.

MARY'S TIPS

Can be made and assembled up to 8 hours ahead.

Freezes well uncooked, without the eggs, for up to 3 weeks.

Cod and Spinach with Gremolata

This is so tasty it will become a go-to weekday supper. Panko breadcrumbs are easy to find and are crisper than regular breadcrumbs. Gremolata is a classic mix of grated lemon, garlic and parsley; we've added breadcrumbs to make it lovely and crisp. The flavours really enhance the dish.

Serves 4

Butter, for greasing
225g (8oz) baby spinach
4 x 150g (5oz) cod loins, skinned
300ml (½ pint) pouring double cream
2 tbsp grainy mustard

For the gremolata

1 tbsp olive oil
30g (1oz) panko breadcrumbs
2 garlic cloves, finely grated
55g (2oz) Parmesan, finely grated
Finely grated zest of 1 lemon
1 tbsp freshly chopped parsley

1. Preheat the oven to 200°C/Fan 180°C/Gas 6. Butter a round 30cm (12in) shallow ovenproof dish.
2. To make the gremolata, heat the oil in a frying pan over a high heat. Add the breadcrumbs and garlic, and fry for a few minutes until lightly golden. Tip into a bowl. Add the Parmesan, lemon zest and parsley, and mix together.
3. Put the spinach leaves into a colander. Pour over a full kettle of boiling water until the spinach has wilted. Refresh under cold water to stop the cooking and keep the bright green colour. Squeeze out as much liquid as you can.
4. Arrange the spinach into four piles on the base of the prepared dish. Place a piece of cod on each pile of spinach and season with salt and freshly ground black pepper.
5. Mix the cream, mustard and a little seasoning together in a small bowl. Divide the sauce between the cod loins, then spoon the gremolata on top. Bake in the preheated oven for about 18–20 minutes (depending on the thickness of the cod loins), until just cooked. The flesh should be white all the way through.
6. Serve piping hot.

MARY'S TIPS

The spinach and cod can be assembled up to 6 hours ahead. Add the sauce and gremolata just before cooking.

Not suitable for freezing.

Lemon Pepper Cod

An all-in-one dish is perfect for making ahead. This can be made with seabass fillets, too, but they can be thinner than cod so may need less time to cook. Choose equal-sized fillets so they cook at the same rate.

Serves 6

Butter, for greasing
6 × 150g (5oz) cod loins, skinned
1 lemon, thinly sliced

For the pepper sauce

2 tbsp olive oil
2 large onions, finely chopped
2 Romano peppers, deseeded and sliced
2 large garlic cloves, finely grated
1 × 400g tin chopped tomatoes
1 tbsp sun-dried tomato paste
2 tbsp capers from a jar, drained

For the herb sauce

115g (4oz) mayonnaise
1 garlic clove, finely grated
1 tbsp freshly chopped dill
1 tbsp freshly chopped parsley
1 tbsp capers from a jar, drained and chopped

1. Preheat the oven to 200°C/Fan 180°C/Gas 6 and butter a wide, shallow ovenproof dish.
2. To make the pepper sauce, heat the olive oil in a frying pan over a medium heat. Add the onions and peppers and fry for about 3–4 minutes. Add the garlic and fry for 10 seconds. Stir in the chopped tomatoes, sun-dried tomato paste and capers, season with salt and freshly ground black pepper, and cover with a lid. Reduce the heat and simmer for about 15 minutes, or until the onions are tender.
3. To make the herb sauce, mix all the ingredients together in a bowl.
4. Spoon the pepper sauce into the prepared ovenproof dish. Top with the cod fillets and season. Spoon the herb sauce on top of the fish, then scatter over the lemon slices. Bake in the preheated oven for about 20–25 minutes, or until the fish is just cooked through and the sauce is bubbling.
5. Serve hot with rice and green vegetables, or with crusty bread and a green salad.

MARY'S TIPS

Can be assembled up to 4 hours ahead.

Not suitable for freezing.

Prawn and Salmon Herb Crumble

Think fish pie with a crunchy topping of breadcrumbs, oats and herbs rather than mashed potato. You can use cod or pollock – whichever you prefer. Deveining prawns can be a faff; leave the vein in if you're short of time. It isn't harmful, just tastier without.

Serves 6

55g (2oz) butter
55g (2oz) plain flour
500ml (18fl oz) hot milk
4 tbsp full-fat mayonnaise
2 tsp Dijon mustard
2 tbsp freshly chopped dill
2 tsp snipped chives
Juice of ½ lemon
55g (2oz) Cheddar, grated
650g (1lb 7oz) salmon, skinned and cut into 3cm (1¼in) cubes
200g (7oz) peeled raw king prawns, deveined (see introduction)

For the topping

175g (6oz) fresh white breadcrumbs
55g (2oz) porridge oats
115g (4oz) butter, melted
1 tbsp freshly chopped dill
55g (2oz) mature Cheddar, grated

1. Preheat the oven to 200°C/Fan 180°C/Gas 6 and grease a fairly shallow 1.7 litre (3 pint) ovenproof dish.
2. Measure the butter into a wide-based saucepan and gently heat until melted. Add the flour and whisk for 30 seconds, then pour in the hot milk, whisking until the sauce is smooth and has thickened.
3. Add the mayonnaise, mustard, herbs, lemon juice and cheese, and stir in well. Add the salmon and prawns and gently simmer for 2 minutes until the prawns just start to turn pink. Season with salt and freshly ground black pepper, then spoon into the ovenproof dish.
4. Mix all the topping ingredients together and season. Sprinkle over the dish in an even layer, then place on a baking sheet to catch any drips. Bake in the oven for about 25 minutes, or until bubbling around the edges, heated through and lightly golden and crisp on top.

MARY'S TIPS

Make up to 8 hours ahead, adding the topping just before baking. You could cook the completed dish in advance and reheat.

Freezes well without the topping. You could freeze it separately and sprinkle over before cooking.

Haddock and Shrimp Feast

A good one pot dish, this is simple to make. It's lovely served in individual bowls simply garnished with green leaves, and it can be eaten just with a fork, so it's ideal for a party.

Serves 4

Knob of butter
1 tbsp sunflower oil
2 onions, roughly chopped
2 celery sticks, finely sliced
1 garlic clove, finely grated
150g (5oz) chestnut mushrooms, thickly sliced
225g (8oz) long-grain rice, rinsed
200ml (⅓ pint) white wine
600ml (1 pint) hot vegetable stock
4 x 125g (4½oz) haddock fillets, skinned weight
150g (5oz) baby spinach
Juice of 1 small lemon
2 tbsp freshly chopped dill
2 tbsp freshly chopped parsley
100ml (3½fl oz) pouring double cream
2 x 55g pots of potted shrimp

1. You will need a deep flameproof and ovenproof casserole, with a lid, that is wide enough for the haddock pieces to sit side by side. Preheat the oven to 180°C/Fan 160°C/Gas 4.
2. Heat the butter and oil in the casserole over a medium heat. Add the onions and celery and fry for a few minutes. Add the garlic and mushrooms to the casserole and stir. Add the rice and stir to coat in the vegetable juices, then fry for a couple more minutes. Pour over the wine and hot stock, then season and bring to the boil.
3. Transfer the dish, uncovered, to the oven and cook for about 10 minutes. Meanwhile, season the pieces of fish.
4. Remove the dish from the oven and sit the haddock on top of the rice – do not overlap the fillets. Bake for another 8–10 minutes until the fish is just done, then transfer the fish to a warm plate. Add the spinach, lemon juice, herbs and cream to the casserole, and stir until the spinach has wilted. Check the seasoning.
5. Warm the potted shrimp in a saucepan until the butter has melted. Return the haddock to the pan, spoon the shrimp over the fish and serve piping hot.

MARY'S TIPS

Best made to serve.

Not suitable for freezing.

Salmon and Fennel One Pot Wonder

So easy to make, yet impressive, this is a really healthy meal for the family. If you're not keen on fennel you could use a thinly sliced medium leek instead, and you could also replace the salmon with pink trout.

Serves 4

Large knob of butter
3 large banana shallots, sliced
1 fennel bulb, core removed, thinly sliced
150ml (¼ pint) white wine
200ml (⅓ pint) full-fat crème fraîche
4 x 125g (4½oz) thin, centre-cut salmon fillets, skinned, each cut in half lengthways (to make 8 thin strips)
115g (4oz) frozen petits pois, defrosted
Squeeze of fresh lemon juice
2 tbsp freshly chopped parsley

1. Melt the butter in a large, wide-based pan over a gentle heat. Add the shallots and fennel and fry over a high heat for about 2–3 minutes. Lower the heat, cover the pan with a lid and continue to cook for about 8–10 minutes until tender.
2. Pour in the wine and boil to reduce by half, then stir in the crème fraîche and bring back to the boil. Season with salt and freshly ground black pepper, then place the salmon strips in a single layer in the sauce. Cover the pan and simmer gently for about 4 minutes until the salmon is nearly cooked.
3. Add the peas, pushing them under the sauce, and continue to cook for about 3 minutes.
4. Stir in the lemon juice, check the seasoning and sprinkle with parsley to serve with crusty bread.

MARY'S TIPS

Best made to serve.

Not suitable for freezing.

Hobie's Tuna Pasta Bake

Hobie and Louis are our grandsons. They love to cook this with me for supper. Not only is it very simple to make but it is also very tasty – both adults and children love it – and is a great last-minute meal as you will probably have all the ingredients in your fridge or storecupboard already.

Serves 4–6

250g (9oz) pasta shapes
4 eggs
55g (2oz) butter
55g (2oz) plain flour
900ml (1½ pints) hot milk
115g (4oz) Cheddar, grated
1 x 185g tin tuna in oil, drained
1 x 195g tin sweetcorn, drained

1. Preheat the oven to 200°C/Fan 180°C/Gas 6.
2. Bring a large pan of salted water to the boil. Add the pasta and cook according to the packet instructions, until tender. Drain well.
3. Meanwhile, cook the eggs in boiling water for 8 minutes, then plunge them into cold water to cool. Remove the egg shells and cut the eggs into quarters.
4. Melt the butter in a small pan over a medium heat. Stir in the flour and cook for 1 minute. Gradually whisk in the milk, stirring until smooth and thickened. Season with salt and freshly ground black pepper, and add most of the cheese.
5. Mix the pasta with the cheese sauce, then add the eggs, flaked tuna and sweetcorn, and turn it into a baking dish. Sprinkle with the remaining cheese, then bake in the preheated oven for 20 minutes until browned.

MARY'S TIPS

This can be prepared up to a day ahead then baked in the oven for about 20 minutes.

This can be frozen for up to 1 month, without the hard-boiled eggs (they will become rubbery when frozen). Sprinkle over the cheese topping after defrosting, just before you bake the dish.

Seafood Linguine with Fresh Tomato Sauce

This recipe tastes of the sea – full of flavour and healthy, too. It is best made and eaten straight away. You can replace the clams with the same weight of mussels, if you prefer.

Serves 6

250g (9oz) dried linguine
3 tbsp olive oil
3 banana shallots, thinly sliced
1 red chilli, deseeded and finely chopped
2 garlic cloves, finely grated
500g (1lb 2oz) fresh live clams, scrubbed (see tip)
250ml (9fl oz) white wine
Juice of ½ lemon
25g (1oz) butter
6 large king scallops, each sliced in half horizontally
150g (5oz) prepared squid, sliced into pieces or rings
150g (5oz) peeled raw king prawns
5 large tomatoes, deseeded and diced
4 tbsp freshly chopped parsley, to garnish

1. Bring a large pan of salted water to the boil. Add the linguine and cook according to the packet instructions, then drain and set aside.
2. Heat the oil in a large, deep frying pan over a high heat, add the shallots, chilli and garlic, and fry for a couple of minutes. Add the clams and fry for a further 5 minutes.
3. Pour in the wine and lemon juice, cover with a lid and cook for 3–4 minutes, until the clams are open (discard any that remain closed).
4. Stir in the drained linguine, season with a little salt and freshly ground black pepper and toss to combine.
5. In a separate pan, melt the butter and fry the scallops over a high heat for 1 minute. Remove with a slotted spoon and add to the pasta. Tip the squid and prawns into the empty pan and fry quickly for about 2 minutes, until just cooked through, then add to the pasta with the cooking juices.
6. Toss everything together over a high heat, add the tomatoes and cook for 1 minute.
7. Pour the seafood linguine into a serving dish, sprinkle over the chopped parsley and serve piping hot.

MARY'S TIPS

When preparing the clams, discard any that remain open when tapped against a work surface.

Best cooked to serve.

Not suitable for freezing.

Chicken and Game

Pesto Lemon Chicken

Chicken Tartiflette

Chicken and Asparagus Fricassee

Whole Roasted Garlic Chicken

Quick Chicken Curry

Easy Peasy One Pot Chicken

Chilli Chicken and Rice Noodle Stir-fry

Mediterranean All-in-one Chicken

Rather Special Chicken Casserole

Tuscan Chicken

Chicken Avocado Bake

Stir-fried Chicken and Vegetable Rice

One Pot Chicken with Pearl Barley and Thyme

Chicken and Bacon Pie

Game Casserole with Cherry and Port Sauce

Two-hour Game Bolognaise

Royal Guineafowl Casserole

Pesto Lemon Chicken

A take on the classic Mediterranean tricolore salad but with cucumber instead of mozzarella and with added chicken. The chicken is best mixed in the dressing a day ahead, to allow the flavours to infuse, while the salad should be made fresh on the day.

Serves 6

3 cooked skinless, boneless chicken breasts, halved horizontally and sliced into thin strips
2 large ripe avocados, peeled and sliced
Juice of ½ large lemon
½ cucumber
175g (6oz) baby plum tomatoes, halved lengthways
30g (1oz) pine nuts, toasted
Micro salad (see tip)
Small bunch of basil, leaves picked

For the dressing
4 tbsp fresh basil pesto
6 tbsp light mayonnaise
Juice of ½ large lemon

1. To make the dressing, measure the pesto, mayonnaise and lemon juice into a large bowl, season with salt and freshly ground black pepper, and mix to combine. Add the chicken and stir again. If possible, leave it to marinate for several hours or in the fridge overnight.
2. Place the avocado slices in a separate bowl, pour over the lemon juice and toss so the avocado is completely coated.
3. Cut the cucumber in half lengthways, use a teaspoon to remove and discard the seeds and then peel using a potato peeler. Cut into crescent-shaped slices and arrange these in layers with the avocado slices, tomato halves and pesto chicken. Check the seasoning.
4. Scatter over the toasted pine nuts, micro salad and basil leaves to finish.

MARY'S TIPS

Micro salad is as it sounds – mini leaves that are pretty and full of flavour. If you can't get hold of it, then a bag of mixed salad leaves or even watercress would make a good alternative.

The dressing can be prepared 1–2 days in advance.

Not suitable for freezing.

Chicken Tartiflette

A take on the classic tartiflette, which is a dish of potato, bacon, onions and Reblochon cheese that is traditional in the Alps. Choose a smoked cured ham of your choice, and waxy potatoes, ideally La Ratte or small new potatoes. If you can't find Reblochon, use Brie or Camembert instead.

Serves 6

- 8 slices Parma or Black Forest ham
- 2 onions, thinly sliced
- 750g (1lb 10oz) waxy potatoes, thickly sliced
- 2 tbsp olive oil
- 2 garlic cloves, finely grated
- 6 small skinless boneless chicken breasts
- 200g (7oz) button mushrooms
- 150ml (¼ pint) white wine
- 150ml (¼ pint) pouring double cream
- 250g (9oz) Reblochon cheese, rind removed and diced
- 1 tbsp grainy mustard
- Juice of ½ lemon
- 1 tbsp freshly chopped thyme

1. Preheat the oven to 200°C/Fan 180°C/Gas 6.
2. Snip two slices of the Parma ham in to small pieces.
3. Put the snipped Parma ham, onions, potatoes, oil and garlic into a large, shallow roasting tin. Season with salt and freshly ground black pepper, and toss everything together. Roast in the preheated oven for about 25 minutes, until the potato slices are nearly tender.
4. Meanwhile, put the remaining slices of Parma ham on a board. Place the chicken breasts on top of the ham and wrap one around each breast. Season.
5. Remove the roasting tin from the oven. Stir in the mushrooms, wine and cream, and add the cheese. Sit the wrapped chicken breasts on top of the vegetables and return to the oven for about 20–22 minutes, or until the chicken is cooked and the vegetables are tender.
6. Remove the chicken from the tin and place on a warm plate to rest. Stir the mustard, lemon juice and thyme into the tin until combined.
7. Carve each chicken breast into three and place over the vegetables and sauce. Serve piping hot.

MARY'S TIPS

The first stage of cooking the vegetables, before adding the chicken, can be made up to 2 hours ahead.

Not suitable for freezing.

Chicken and Asparagus Fricassee

A speedy, French-inspired stew with fresh herbs and that queen of green vegetables – asparagus. Oyster mushrooms are tender and therefore best kept in large pieces so they retain their charm. If they're not available, another exotic mushroom, such as shiitake, will work well, as will standard closed-cup or chestnut mushrooms.

Serves 4

3 tbsp olive oil

250g (9oz) oyster mushrooms, halved

4 skinless and boneless chicken breasts (about 150g/5oz each), sliced into thick pieces (see tip)

2 tbsp runny honey

1 medium leek, thinly sliced

1 garlic clove, finely grated

200ml (⅓ pint) white wine

300ml (½ pint) pouring double cream

200g (7oz) asparagus spears, stalks sliced into rounds and tips kept whole

1 tbsp freshly chopped mint

1 tbsp freshly chopped basil

1. Heat 1 tablespoon of the oil in a large frying pan over a high heat. Add the mushrooms, season with salt and pepper and fry for 3–4 minutes until golden and any liquid has evaporated. Remove from the pan and set aside on a plate.

2. Heat another tablespoon of oil in the pan. Season the chicken pieces and toss in the runny honey to coat. Add the chicken to the pan and fry over a medium-high heat for 4–6 minutes until just cooked. Remove from the pan and set aside.

3. Add the remaining oil and the leek to the pan and fry gently for 3–5 minutes over a low heat until softened. Stir in the garlic and fry for 30 seconds. Pour in the wine and boil for 2–3 minutes to reduce by half, then stir in the cream and cook for another minute or so to reduce slightly – it will be a thin sauce.

4. Return the fried chicken pieces and mushrooms to the pan and simmer for a few minutes until heated through and the chicken is fully cooked, with no traces of pink in the middle.

5. Meanwhile, cook the asparagus stalks and tips in the boiling salted water for 2–3 minutes. Drain and add to the chicken with the herbs. Season to taste and serve piping hot.

MARY'S TIPS

You can keep the chicken breasts whole, if you prefer, but they will take longer to cook.

Can be made a day ahead without the asparagus. Reheat, then stir in the freshly cooked asparagus.

The cooked dish can be frozen without the asparagus.

Whole Roasted Garlic Chicken

If you have any lemon shells left over after using their juice for another recipe, use them instead of the fresh lemon wedges. Baby courgettes are firmer than large fat ones; they might not brown after 20 minutes but stay bright green, which is lovely.

Serves 6

1 x 1.75kg (4lb) chicken
1 lemon, cut into 6 wedges
A good sprig of thyme

For the garlic butter
55g (2oz) butter, softened
2 fat garlic cloves, finely grated

For the vegetables
250g (9oz) shallots, peeled
500g (1lb 2oz) small carrots
2 parsnips, peeled and cut into thick slices
150g (5½oz) baby courgettes, sliced lengthways
2 tbsp olive oil

For the gravy
2 heaped tbsp plain flour
100ml (3½fl oz) white wine
400ml (14fl oz) chicken stock

To garnish
Small handful of parsley sprigs

1. You will need a large roasting tin for the chicken, large enough to hold the vegetables in a single layer, as well as the chicken. Preheat the oven to 200°C/Fan 180°C/Gas 6.
2. Mix the butter and garlic together and season with salt and pepper. Spread the garlic butter over the skin over the breasts. Stuff the cavity with the lemon wedges and thyme sprig, then place the chicken in a roasting tin. Season with salt and pepper and roast in the preheated oven for about 20 minutes.
3. Toss the prepared vegetables, except the courgettes, in the oil and season. Scatter the vegetables around the chicken in the roasting tin. Return to the oven for 40 minutes.
4. Finally, add the courgettes to the tin and return the tray to the oven. Roast for a further 20 minutes, or until the vegetables are golden and the chicken is tender, basting from time to time with the juices.
5. Transfer the chicken to a carving board to rest, and spoon the vegetables into a dish and keep warm. Sit the roasting tin over a low heat on the hob, sprinkle in the flour and whisk, scraping up the sides of the tin. Blend in the wine and stock and bring to the boil, stirring until thickened.
6. Carve or joint the chicken and serve with the vegetables and gravy, garnished with parsley.

MARY'S TIPS

Cover the prepared chicken with clingfilm and pile the prepared vegetables in a bowl and cover. Both can be kept in the fridge for up to 24 hours before roasting. Make sure that the chicken is at room temperature before cooking.

Quick Chicken Curry

This curry is full of flavour, hence the long list of ingredients – though traditional versions have many more than this!

Serves 4–6

3 tbsp sunflower oil
4 large skinless chicken breasts, sliced into 2cm (¾in) strips
2 large onions, finely chopped
1 tbsp finely grated fresh root ginger
2 garlic cloves, finely grated
½ red chilli, deseeded and finely chopped
½ tsp ground cardamom
¼ tsp ground cloves
1 tbsp medium curry powder
1 tbsp turmeric
1 tsp ground cumin
1 tbsp plain flour
450ml (¾ pint) chicken stock
2 tbsp mango chutney
100ml (3½fl oz) full-fat plain yoghurt or double cream
Handful of coriander leaves, to garnish (optional)

1. Heat 2 tablespoons of the oil in a deep frying pan over a high heat. Season the chicken strips with salt and freshly ground black pepper and brown quickly all over until sealed (you may need to do this in batches). Remove with a slotted spoon to a plate.
2. Add the onions to the pan and fry for a few minutes, then cover, lower the heat and fry for 10 minutes, until softened.
3. Remove the lid, increase the heat and add the ginger, garlic and chilli, and fry for 1 minute. Sprinkle in the ground spices and fry for a few minutes more. Sprinkle in the flour, then stir in the stock and bring to the boil until thickened.
4. Add the mango chutney and return the chicken to the pan. Lower the heat, cover and simmer for 5–10 minutes, or until the chicken is cooked through and tender.
5. Check the seasoning, then add the yoghurt or cream and serve hot, sprinkled with coriander, if using, with naan bread or rice.

MARY'S TIPS

The curry can be made without adding the yoghurt up to 1 day ahead. Reheat gently to serve and stir in the yoghurt.

The curry freezes well without the yoghurt.

Easy Peasy One Pot Chicken

A whole spatchcock chicken with Mediterranean-style vegetables, this is a healthy and hearty all-in-one dish. Removing the backbone of the chicken makes it a spatchcock and it is easier to arrange in the pot and to carve or joint. Double up for more people, if you wish, and arrange two chickens in a large roasting tin, covered in foil.

Serves 4

2 tbsp olive oil
1 large onion, thinly sliced
1 large fennel bulb, thinly sliced
1 red pepper, deseeded and diced
3 large garlic cloves, finely grated
100ml (3½fl oz) white wine
1 × 400g tin chopped tomatoes
2 tbsp sun-dried tomato paste
2 tsp Worcestershire sauce
1 small whole chicken (about 1.25kg/2lb 12oz)
1 lemon, thinly sliced
5 bay leaves
Pinch of paprika
1 tbsp honey

1. Preheat the oven to 200°C/Fan 180°C/Gas 6.
2. Heat the oil in a flameproof casserole or ovenproof frying pan that has a lid over a high heat. Add the onion, fennel and pepper and fry for about 3–4 minutes. Add the garlic and fry for 30 seconds. Pour in the wine and bubble to reduce by half.
3. Stir in the chopped tomatoes, sun-dried tomato paste and Worcestershire sauce, and season with salt and freshly ground black pepper.
4. Meanwhile, put the chicken upside down on a board. Remove the backbone by cutting either side of the bone with scissors. Turn over and press down on the breast bone to flatten the bird; it is now a spatchcock chicken.
5. Put the chicken, breast-side up, on the vegetables in the casserole or pan. Arrange the lemon slices and bay leaves over the chicken, then season and bring up to the boil. Cover with a lid and transfer to the preheated oven for about 35 minutes.
6. Remove the lid and sprinkle the paprika over the chicken and drizzle with the honey. Return to the oven, uncovered, for about 30 minutes to brown and finish cooking.
7. To serve, spoon the vegetables on to a hot platter and joint or carve the chicken before resting on top.

MARY'S TIPS

Prepare the vegetables ahead. Bring the veg back to the boil before adding the chicken and cooking in the oven.

Not suitable for freezing.

Chilli Chicken and Rice Noodle Stir-fry

Quick, healthy and bursting with flavour, this is a great dish to teach teenagers to make, as they'll enjoy the results. Peas are fine to add frozen; they will instantly defrost in the hot stir-fry.

Serves 4–6

175g (6oz) thin rice noodles
2 small skinless chicken breasts, sliced into strips
2 tbsp sweet chilli sauce
4 tbsp soy sauce
1 tbsp light muscovado sugar
1 garlic clove, finely grated
Juice of 1 lime
2 tbsp sunflower oil
115g (4oz) baby corn, sliced in half lengthways
1 red onion, finely sliced
1 red chilli, thinly sliced
150g (5oz) sugar snap peas, destringed, if necessary, and thinly sliced
75g (3oz) frozen petits pois
Small bunch of coriander, leaves chopped
75g (3oz) cashew nuts, chopped and toasted

1. Cook the noodles in a pan of boiling water according to the packet instructions. Drain, run under cold water, then drain again.
2. Season the chicken with salt and black pepper, tip into a bowl and coat in 1 tablespoon of the sweet chilli sauce.
3. Mix the remaining chilli sauce with the soy, sugar, garlic and lime juice in a small bowl.
4. Place a large frying pan or wok over a high heat until hot. Add 1 tablespoon of the oil and fry the chicken until golden and just cooked through. Remove from the pan and set aside.
5. Add the remaining oil, baby corn, red onion, chilli and sugar snap peas to the pan. Fry over a high heat for 2 minutes. Add the frozen peas, cooked noodles, coriander, cooked chicken and the sauce mixture. Toss over the heat for few minutes until piping hot.
6. Add the coriander, toss well and check the seasoning. Sprinkle with the cashew nuts to serve.

MARY'S TIPS

Best made and served.

Not suitable for freezing.

Mediterranean All-in-one Chicken

This is a great way to feed the family, with the chicken and veg all cooked in one very large tray in the oven (see tip). It takes only minutes to put everything together, then it sits in the oven for under an hour with no fussy finishing off to do and only one pan to wash up. The recipe allows one chicken thigh and one drumstick per person. I love stuffed olives, but use plain green or black ones, if you prefer. The preserved lemons really give a lovely citrus tang to the dish and are well worth using, but if you can't find them use one sliced lemon instead. Traditionally from Morocco, the lemons are preserved in salt water and are beautifully soft and citrusy. Use them to flavour tagines and chicken or pork dishes. They will keep in the jar in the fridge for 1 month, or you can freeze them for up to 3 months.

Serves 6

1kg (2lb 4oz) main crop potatoes, peeled and cut into 5cm (2in) chunks

3 tbsp olive oil

1 large onion, cut into wedges

2 garlic cloves, finely grated

6 rashers of smoked streaky bacon, snipped into 1cm (½in) pieces

6 chicken thighs

6 chicken drumsticks

5 preserved lemons, cut into quarters (see introduction)

1½ tsp paprika

3 courgettes, thickly sliced

1 × 200g tin anchovy-stuffed green olives, drained

1. Preheat the oven to 220°C/Fan 200°C/Gas 7.
2. Place the potatoes in a large roasting tin with 2 tablespoons of the oil. Toss well to coat the potatoes in the oil. Add the onion, garlic, bacon and chicken pieces and toss together. Add the lemons, season everything well with salt and freshly ground black pepper, and sprinkle with the paprika. Roast in the preheated oven for 40 minutes.
3. Meanwhile, in a bowl, toss the courgettes in the remaining tablespoon of oil and season.
4. Remove the roasting tin from the oven and poke the courgette slices in among the chicken, then scatter the olives over the top. Return to the oven for a further 20 minutes, until the chicken and vegetables are golden brown and tender.

MARY'S TIPS

Don't overcrowd the roasting tin; you need everything to be in a single layer or it will not cook evenly – divide between two tins, if necessary.

Best made and served.

Not suitable for freezing.

Rather Special Chicken Casserole

An all-in-one dish to cook and serve. Sage is readily available fresh and is simple to grow. It comes with either grey or purple leaves – they both taste the same.

Serves 4–6

250g (9oz) streaky bacon, snipped into small pieces
2 large onions, roughly chopped
8 skinless bone-in chicken thighs
2 tbsp sunflower oil
30g (1oz) plain flour
150ml (¼ pint) hot chicken stock
150ml (¼ pint) white wine
2 large sprigs of thyme
Small bunch of sage, 6 leaves removed for garnish
2 bay leaves
200g (7oz) chestnut mushrooms, quartered
115g (4oz) full-fat crème fraîche
Knob of butter
Small bunch of parsley, leaves chopped

1. Preheat the oven to 160°C/Fan 140°C/Gas 3.
2. Place the bacon in a large ovenproof frying pan that has a lid or flameproof casserole and fry over a medium heat for a few minutes. Add the onions and continue to fry until the bacon is brown at the edges. Transfer the bacon and onions to a plate using a slotted spoon and set aside.
3. Lightly season the chicken. Place the oil in the unwashed pan, add the chicken and brown over a high heat, turning once. Transfer to the plate with the bacon and onions.
4. Scatter the flour into the pan (adding a little more oil, if needed) and stir to combine. Gradually incorporate the hot stock, whisking, and allow to thicken. Pour in the wine and return the bacon, onions and chicken to the pan. Stir well, add the thyme sprigs, sage sprigs and bay leaves. The sauce will be quite thick at this stage. Bring to the boil and season well with salt and black pepper. Cover with a lid, transfer to the oven and cook for 30 minutes.
5. Remove the dish from the oven and add the mushrooms and crème fraîche. Stir well and return to the oven for a further 15–20 minutes, until the chicken is tender.
6. Meanwhile, heat the butter in a small pan over a medium heat. Add the whole sage leaves and fry until crisp.
7. Remove the bay, thyme and sage sprigs from the casserole and discard (some leaves may have fallen off). Stir in the parsley and serve with the crisp sage leaves on top.

MARY'S TIPS

Can be made 1 day ahead. Add the crème fraîche and mushrooms when reheating.

Freezes well.

Tuscan Chicken

Based on a classic, this is one of our favourites for an easy supper. Use chicken breasts, if you prefer.

Serves 6

- 6 large skinless bone-in chicken thighs
- 2 tbsp plain flour
- 2 tsp paprika
- 2 tbsp olive or sunflower oil
- 1 large onion, finely chopped
- 1 large red pepper, deseeded and finely diced
- 2 garlic cloves, finely grated
- 2 tsp tomato purée
- 30g (1oz) sun-blushed tomatoes, chopped
- 150ml (¼ pint) white wine
- 150ml (¼ pint) chicken stock
- 150ml (¼ pint) pouring double cream
- 150g (5oz) baby spinach
- 55g (2oz) Parmesan, grated

1. Place the chicken thighs in a bowl. Add the flour and half the paprika and season well with salt and freshly ground black pepper. Toss together to coat.
2. Heat the oil in a large, deep frying pan over a high heat. Add the chicken and fry for 3–4 minutes on each side, until browned and crisp. Set aside on a plate.
3. Add the onion and pepper to the unwashed pan and fry for 4–5 minutes over a medium heat, until soft. You may need a little more oil. Add the garlic and fry for 30 seconds.
4. Stir in the tomato purée, sun-blushed tomatoes, wine and stock and bring up to the boil. Return the chicken to the pan with any resting juices, cover, reduce the heat and simmer for about 30 minutes, until tender.
5. Add the cream and spinach to the pan and stir until wilted. Remove from the heat, sprinkle with the cheese and serve piping hot.

MARY'S TIPS

Can be made up to a day ahead.

Freezes well.

Chicken Avocado Bake

This is a variation of an American chicken salad that I have made for years. It is quick, easy and very, very delicious! Serve with a green salad and crusty bread.

Serves 4–6

2 celery sticks, thinly sliced
4 spring onions, sliced
300ml (½ pint) full-fat mayonnaise
Juice of 1 small lemon
100g (3½oz) mature Cheddar, grated
1 large just-ripe avocado, peeled and cut into cubes (see tip)
350g (12oz) cooked chicken, cut into small cubes (see tip)
225g (8oz) cherry tomatoes, halved
1 x 45g packet of ready-salted crisps, crushed into tiny crumbs
Paprika, for sprinkling

1. You will need a 1.5 litre (2½ pint) wide-based, shallow ovenproof dish. Preheat the oven to 200°C/Fan 180°C/Gas 6.
2. Tip the celery and spring onions into a large bowl, then add the mayonnaise, half the lemon juice and two-thirds of the grated cheese. Season with salt and pepper and mix together.
3. Toss the avocado cubes in the remaining lemon juice, then add to the bowl, along with the chicken. Carefully mix everything together, then spoon into the ovenproof dish.
4. Scatter over the tomatoes, making sure they are near the centre of the dish, as they may overcook at the edges. Sprinkle the remaining cheese, the crushed crisps and paprika over the top.
5. Bake in the preheated oven for 12–15 minutes until golden and piping hot in the middle (see tip). As it takes such a short time to cook, it is best served straight from the oven.

MARY'S TIPS

Choose an avocado that is firm and just ripe, otherwise the cubes will not keep their shape.

Can be assembled up to 12 hours ahead, but sprinkle with the crisps and bake to serve.

Not suitable for freezing.

Stir-fried Chicken and Vegetable Rice

Healthy and all in one, the perfect midweek supper.

Serves 4–6

- 2 skinless and boneless chicken breasts, sliced into small strips/diced
- 3 tbsp sunflower oil
- 2 large banana shallots, finely sliced
- 1 large red pepper, deseeded and diced
- 200g (7oz) button mushrooms, sliced
- 150g (5oz) beansprouts
- 2 × 250g packets cooked long-grain rice
- 100g (3½oz) frozen petits pois
- 1 bunch of spring onions, sliced

For the marinade and sauce

- 2 garlic cloves, finely grated
- Small piece fresh root ginger, peeled and grated
- 6 tbsp soy sauce
- 3 tbsp sweet chilli sauce
- 1 tbsp runny honey

1. Measure all the marinade ingredients into a jug. Mix well, then pour half into a large bowl, keeping the remaining marinade in the jug. Add the chicken to the bowl and stir to coat. Leave to marinate for 30 minutes, or longer if possible.
2. Heat 2 tablespoons of the oil in a large frying pan over a high heat. Add the chicken and fry over a high heat until golden all over and just cooked. Remove with a slotted spoon and set aside.
3. Add the remaining oil, the shallots and pepper to the pan, and fry for a few minutes. Add the mushrooms and beansprouts, and fry for a few minutes, until the beansprouts are wilted.
4. Meanwhile, reheat the packets of rice according to the packet instructions. Tip the rice into the pan, then add the petits pois and spring onions.
5. Return the chicken to the pan and pour in the reserved marinade. Toss everything over the heat and serve immediately.

MARY'S TIPS

Best made and served.

Not suitable for freezing.

One Pot Chicken with Pearl Barley and Thyme

All cooked in one pot, this healthy chicken and pearl barley dish is a great one to feed a gang and is high in fibre, too.

Serves 6

- 1 tbsp sunflower oil
- 8 skinless bone-in chicken thighs
- 1 large onion, roughly chopped
- 2 carrots, diced
- 2 large garlic cloves, finely grated
- 225g (8oz) pearl barley
- 200ml (⅓ pint) white wine
- 700ml (1¼ pints) chicken stock
- 3 sprigs of thyme
- 125g (4½oz) frozen petits pois
- Juice of ½ lemon
- Small bunch of parsley, leaves chopped

1. Preheat the oven to 150°C/Fan 130°C/Gas 2.
2. Place the oil in a wide-based ovenproof frying pan or flameproof casserole over a high heat. Season the chicken thighs and brown them on all sides, until golden. Remove from the pan and set aside.
3. Add the onion and carrots to the pan and fry for a few minutes. Add the garlic and fry for 30 seconds. Stir in the pearl barley and pour in the wine. Bring to the boil and allow the wine to reduce for a few seconds. Add the stock and thyme sprigs, cover with a lid and boil for 10 minutes.
4. Return the chicken to the pan, transfer the dish, uncovered, to the oven and cook for about 50–60 minutes, until the pearl barley is tender. Add the petits pois and lemon juice for the final 5 minutes of the cooking time.
5. Remove the thyme sprigs, sprinkle with the chopped parsley and serve hot.

MARY'S TIPS

Use as wide-based a pan as possible, so the liquid can reduce. If you use a small pan, you may have a little excess liquid at the end of the cooking time.

Best made and served.

Not suitable for freezing.

Chicken and Bacon Pie

This pie would make a wonderful centrepiece for a family meal or other gathering. My granddaughters Abby and Grace helped me to make it for a TV programme. Using bought puff pastry is much easier and quicker than making your own.

Serves 6

55g (2oz) butter

1 large onion, roughly chopped

4 celery sticks, diced

250g (9oz) smoked back bacon (about 7 rashers), cut into small pieces

250g (9oz) chestnut mushrooms, halved

60g (2½oz) plain flour, plus extra for dusting

110ml (3¾fl oz) white wine

450ml (¾ pint) chicken stock

2 tbsp full-fat crème fraîche

1 tbsp grainy mustard

500g (1lb 2oz) cooked chicken, cut into pieces

1 × 375g packet ready-rolled, all-butter puff pastry

1 egg, beaten

1. You will need a 2 litre (3½ pint) shallow, wide-based ovenproof dish with a lip, about 25 × 33 × 6cm (10 × 13 × 2¼in). Preheat the oven to 200°C/Fan 180°C/Gas 6.

2. Melt the butter in a frying pan. Add the onion, celery and bacon, and fry over a high heat for a few minutes. Cover, reduce the heat and cook for about 10 minutes until soft.

3. Add the mushrooms, increase the heat and fry for a few minutes. Sprinkle in the flour slowly and stir. Slowly pour in the wine and stock, stirring all the time, until smooth. Simmer for a few minutes and stir until thickened. Add the crème fraîche, mustard and chicken and season with salt and pepper. Spoon into the oven dish and leave to cool.

4. Unroll the pastry on to a floured work surface and roll to a little bigger than the dish. Sit a pie funnel in the centre of the dish and wet the lip of the dish. Place the pastry on the top of the dish, pushing the pie funnel through. Press the pastry firmly against the lip to secure and score the top in a diamond pattern. Brush with the beaten egg.

5. Bake in the oven for 30 minutes until the pastry is golden and cooked through, and the chicken is bubbling. Serve hot.

MARY'S TIPS

The pie filling can be prepared up to a day ahead. The dish freezes well without the pastry. Defrost to room temperature, top with pastry and cook to serve.

Game Casserole with Cherry and Port Sauce

This is an intensely flavoured stew, rich and full-bodied, that really benefits from being made ahead as the taste improves with keeping. If you don't have any cherry jam, redcurrant jelly makes a good substitute.

Serves 6

- 2 tbsp sunflower oil
- 1kg (2lb 4oz) stewing game, cut into 2cm (¾in) cubes
- 2 leeks, thickly sliced
- 2 celery sticks, thinly sliced
- 40g (1½oz) plain flour
- 300ml (½ pint) Port
- 500ml (18fl oz) game or beef stock
- 3 bay leaves
- 2 star anise
- 1 tbsp cherry jam

1. Heat the oil in a large flameproof casserole or deep frying pan that has a lid over a high heat. Season the game with salt and freshly ground black pepper, then add to the pan and fry until well browned – you may need to do this in batches. Remove the game with a slotted spoon and set aside.
2. Add the leeks and celery to the pan and fry over a high heat for 1 minute. Sprinkle in the flour and continue to fry, stirring constantly, for a further minute. Gradually pour in the Port and the stock, stirring all the time, and bring to the boil. Allow to boil for 2–3 minutes until thickened, then add the bay leaves, star anise and cherry jam.
3. Return the game to the pan and bring back to the boil. Lower the heat, cover with a lid and simmer over a low heat for about 2 hours, stirring occasionally, until tender.
4. Remove the bay leaf and star anise, and check the seasoning to serve.

MARY'S TIPS

The casserole can be made up to 3 days ahead and reheated to serve.

The cooked dish freezes well.

Two-hour Game Bolognaise

Unlike a beef bolognaise, this has a deep gamey flavour and needs long, slow cooking. You can buy game casserole packs in supermarkets. If buying from your local butcher, ask for a mixture of your favourite game – pheasant, guinea fowl, rabbit, venison, partridge.

Serves 6

3 tbsp sunflower oil
750g (1lb 10oz) mixed game meat, cut into 2cm (¾in) cubes
1 large onion, roughly chopped
2 small carrots, finely chopped
150g (5oz) chestnut mushrooms, finely diced
2 garlic cloves, finely grated
1 tbsp light muscovado sugar
2 tbsp tomato purée
300ml (½ pint) red wine
1 × 400g tin chopped tomatoes
200ml (⅓ pint) beef stock
1 tbsp finely chopped rosemary leaves
3 bay leaves
500g (1lb 2oz) spaghetti
Freshly grated Parmesan, to serve

1. Preheat the oven to 150°C/Fan 130°C/Gas 2.
2. Heat the oil in a large, ovenproof frying pan that has a lid, or a flameproof casserole over a high heat. Add the diced meat and cook, in batches, if necessary, until golden and sealed. Transfer to a plate with a slotted spoon and set aside.
3. Add the onion and carrots to the pan, plus a little extra oil, if needed, and fry over a high heat for about 5 minutes, until starting to brown. Add the mushrooms and garlic and fry for a further 5 minutes, until the mushrooms have softened.
4. Return the game to the pan, sprinkle in the sugar, add the tomato purée and fry for 1 minute. Pour in the wine, chopped tomatoes and stock. Add the herbs and season with salt and freshly ground black pepper. Bring to the boil, then cover with a lid and transfer to the oven to cook for about 2 hours, or until the meat is falling apart (see tip). Add a little more stock at this point if the bolognaise is looking a little dry.
5. Shortly before the bolognaise has finished cooking, bring a pan of salted water to the boil and cook the spaghetti according to the packet instructions. Drain well, transfer to plates and serve with the bolognaise spooned on top, and a sprinkling of grated Parmesan.

MARY'S TIPS

This is all about long, slow cooking. As different meats are being used, they need to cook for a long time until each of them is falling apart and tender.

The bolognaise can be made up to 2 days ahead and reheated to serve. Freezes well cooked.

Royal Guineafowl Casserole

With its tarragon mushroom sauce, this casserole would grace any royal feast. This recipe is also good made with chicken thighs or breasts.

Serves 4

1 large guineafowl
2 tbsp sunflower oil
30g (1oz) butter
500g (1lb 2oz) shallots, thickly sliced
2 garlic cloves, finely grated
1 tsp light muscovado sugar
2 tsp balsamic vinegar
500g (1lb 2oz) chestnut mushrooms, halved
30g (1oz) plain flour
300ml (½ pint) white wine
100ml (3½fl oz) pouring double cream
2 tbsp chopped tarragon

MARY'S TIPS

If you're unsure about jointing the guineafowl, ask your butcher to do this for you.

The casserole can be made up to a day ahead, adding the tarragon to serve. Freezes well. Omit the tarragon and add to serve.

1. Preheat the oven to 160°C/Fan 140°C/Gas 3.
2. Joint the guineafowl and remove the legs (the whole leg, with the thigh and drumstick in one piece) and breast from the bone, so you have two legs and two breasts (see tip). Skin the joints, then season with salt and pepper.
3. Heat 1 tablespoon of the oil and half the butter in a deep ovenproof frying pan that has a lid or a flameproof casserole. When the butter has melted, brown the joints over a high heat until golden all over – you may need to do this in batches. Remove from the pan and set aside.
4. Add the remining oil, if needed, tip in the shallots and fry over a high heat, stirring frequently, for 4–5 minutes. Add the garlic, sugar and vinegar and fry for another 2–3 minutes until the shallots start to become golden. Add the mushrooms to the casserole and fry for a few minutes.
5. Measure the flour into a large bowl and gradually whisk in the wine, a little at a time, until you have a smooth paste, then add the rest to make a cloudy liquid. Pour into the pan and stir over the heat until thickened and smooth. Season with salt and pepper, then return the leg joints to the pan.
6. Bring to the boil, cover with a lid and transfer to the oven to cook for about 20 minutes.
7. Add the breasts, mixing them into the sauce, and return to the oven to cook for a further 15 minutes, or until tender.
8. Stir in the cream and add the tarragon, then check the seasoning. Serve piping hot.

Pork, Beef and Lamb

All-in-one Sausage and Egg Breakfast

Meatball Toad in the Hole with Sage

Pappardelle with Tomato and Vodka Sauce

Spicy Pork with Sweet Potato and Black-eyed Beans

One Tray Sausage Supper

Thai Basil Beef Stir-fry

Swiss Herb Beef and Potato Gratin

Scrumpy Beef Casserole with Parsley and Horseradish Dumplings

Cottage Pie with Crushed Potato Topping

Mexican Tortilla Bake

Beef and Ale Casserole with Pickled Walnuts

Lamb Tagine

Sweet Smoked Paprika Lamb with Borlotti Beans

Minted Lamb Casserole with Porcini Mushrooms

French Slow-roast Lamb with Ratatouille

All-in-one Sausage and Egg Breakfast

An all-in-one breakfast dish to serve four hungry teenagers or indeed anyone with a hearty appetite! It's also a great way to cook breakfast in a hurry – with much less washing-up too. Perfect hangover food, or so I am told!

Serves 4

8 good-quality pork sausages or 1–2 Cumberland rings (see tip)

1 tbsp sunflower oil

2 large just-ripe tomatoes, quartered

250g (9oz) large field mushrooms, thickly sliced

4 large eggs

2 tbsp finely snipped chives

1. Preheat the oven to 200°C/Fan 180°C/Gas 6.
2. Place the sausages in a large roasting tin, add the oil and toss together. Roast in the preheated oven for about 15–20 minutes, or until the sausages are golden underneath.
3. Turn the sausages over, scatter with the tomatoes and mushrooms, and season with salt and freshly ground black pepper. Return to the oven to cook for another 10 minutes.
4. Crack the eggs into the roasting tin and return to the oven for a further 4–5 minutes, or until just set. Sprinkle with the chives and serve with buttered toast.

MARY'S TIPS

If you use chipolata or cocktail sausages, this will take less time to cook – about 20 minutes in total.

Best made and served at once.

Not suitable for freezing.

Meatball Toad in the Hole with Sage

Think of a classic toad in the hole, then replace the sausages with herbed meatballs. You could also make it in a small roasting tin, but it makes a nice change to cook it in a round pan.

Serves 6

350g (12oz) pork sausage meat
30g (1oz) Parmesan, grated
1 tbsp freshly chopped sage
1 tsp Dijon mustard
4 spring onions, finely chopped
4 tbsp plain flour
6 tbsp sunflower oil

For the batter
115g (4oz) plain flour
4 large eggs
150ml (¼ pint) milk

1. Preheat the oven to 240°C/Fan 220°C/Gas 9.
2. Put the sausage meat, Parmesan, sage, mustard and spring onions into a bowl. Season well with salt and freshly ground black pepper and, using your hands, knead together to mix the flavours. Shape into 20 equal-sized meatballs, then roll in the plain flour.
3. To make the batter, measure the flour into a bowl and make a little well in the centre. Break the eggs into the well and add a little of the milk. Whisk by hand, slowly adding the rest of the milk, until you have a smooth batter.
4. Heat 1 tablespoon of the oil in an ovenproof non-stick frying pan. Add the meatballs and brown over a high heat. Remove the meatballs from the pan and set aside.
5. Add the remaining oil to the pan and put the pan in the oven for 10 minutes to get hot.
6. When the oil is very hot, pour in the batter and place the meatballs on top. Bake in the oven for about 25–30 minutes, until well risen and the batter is golden brown and crisp.

MARY'S TIPS

Brown the meatballs and mix the batter up to 6 hours ahead.

Meatballs freeze well uncooked.

Pappardelle with Tomato and Vodka Sauce

Rather an adult sauce! This recipe is the formula for relaxing everyone and getting a party going with a swing. If you can't get pappardelle, try making it with tagliatelle or fettuccine instead.

Serves 4–6

25g (1oz) butter
1 onion, finely chopped
2 garlic cloves, finely grated
1 × 400g tin chopped tomatoes
115g (4oz) Parma, Black Forest or Serrano ham, chopped
150ml (¼ pint) vodka
1 × 200g carton full-fat crème fraîche
Small handful of basil leaves
40g (1½oz) Parmesan, grated, plus extra to serve
400–450g (14–16oz) dried pappardelle
Good handful of fresh parsley, roughly chopped

1. Melt the butter in a deep frying pan over a medium-high heat. Add the onion and garlic and fry for about 5 minutes, until the onion is quite brown.

2. Pour in the tinned tomatoes and stir in the ham. Leave the mixture to simmer gently, uncovered, for about 10 minutes. Pour in the vodka and simmer, uncovered, for a further 5 minutes.

3. Add the crème fraîche and basil leaves and carry on simmering for 5–10 minutes, or until the mixture is a good consistency for coating pasta. Remove the sauce from the heat and add the Parmesan. Taste and season with salt and freshly ground black pepper, if needed.

4. Meanwhile, cook the pasta in boiling salted water according to the packet instructions, until al dente. Drain and quickly toss the pasta in the pan with the sauce, adding a spoonful of pasta water to loosen, if needed.

5. Sprinkle with the parsley and serve immediately with additional Parmesan.

MARY'S TIP

The sauce can be made ahead, quickly cooled, covered and kept in the fridge for up to 2 days. Bring to the boil in a pan before serving with the freshly boiled pasta.

The sauce freezes well.

Spicy Pork with Sweet Potato and Black-eyed Beans

A great stew to make ahead, and perfect for sharing.

Serves 6

1 tbsp sunflower oil
1kg (2lb 4oz) pork shoulder, cut into about 2.5cm (1in) pieces
2 large onions, thinly sliced
1 green pepper, deseeded and diced
2 large garlic cloves, finely grated
½–1 red chilli, deseeded and finely chopped
1 tbsp each of ground cumin, ground coriander and paprika
2 × 400g tins chopped tomatoes
200ml (⅓ pint) chicken stock
2 tbsp tomato purée
2 tsp caster sugar
1 × 400g tin black-eyed beans, drained and rinsed
1 large sweet potato, peeled and cut into 2cm (¾in) cubes

1. Preheat the oven to 150°C/Fan 130°C/Gas 2.

2. Heat the oil in a large ovenproof frying pan that has a lid or a flameproof casserole over a high heat. Add the pork and fry in batches for 3–4 minutes, until sealed and browned. Remove with a slotted spoon and set aside.

3. Add the onions and pepper to the pan and fry for 5 minutes, until softened. Add the garlic, chilli and spices and fry for a few seconds, then stir in the tomatoes, stock, purée and sugar.

4. Return the pork and any resting juices to the pan and season with salt and freshly ground black pepper. Bring up to the boil, stirring, then cover with a lid and transfer to the oven for about 1 hour.

5. Add the rinsed beans and the sweet potato to the stew and return to the oven for 30–45 minutes, or until the pork is tender and the sweet potato is cooked.

MARY'S TIPS

Can be made up to 2 days ahead; add the beans and sweet potato and finish cooking for 30–45 minutes when reheating.

Freezes well without the beans and sweet potato.

One Tray Sausage Supper

An all-in-one dish with root veg and your favourite sausages. Perfect with the big fat butcher's variety.

Serves 4–6

500g (1lb 2oz) Chantenay carrots (scrubbed or peeled, as needed)
1kg (2lb 4oz) large potatoes, peeled and cut into 2.5cm (1in) cubes
2 tbsp sunflower oil
55g (2oz) butter
2 large onions, sliced
2 garlic cloves, finely grated
12 good butcher's pork sausages
55g (2oz) Parmesan, coarsely grated

1. Preheat the oven to 220°C/Fan 200°C/Gas 7.
2. Bring a saucepan of salted water to the boil. Add the carrots and potatoes and boil for about 4 minutes, then drain well.
3. Meanwhile, place the oil and butter in a large roasting tin and heat in the oven. Add the drained vegetables to the tin with the onions and garlic, season with salt and pepper, and toss in the hot oil. Arrange the sausages on top.
4. Roast in the oven for about 20 minutes, or until the tops of the sausages are brown. Turn the sausages over and roast for a further 15 minutes, or until the vegetables are golden and tender and the sausages are crisp. Remove the sausages and leave to rest on a plate, loosely covered with foil, to keep warm.
5. Turn the vegetables over, sprinkle with the cheese and cook in the oven for a final 10 minutes to brown the veg. Return the sausages to the tin and serve piping hot.

MARY'S TIPS

Keep the vegetables in a simple layer so they stay crisp and do not become soggy.

Not suitable for freezing.

Thai Basil Beef Stir-fry

Quick, easy and all in one dish. Mint would work well with this dish, if you can't find Thai basil.

Serves 6

350g (12oz) rump steak, sliced into long strips
1 red chilli, deseeded and finely chopped
Juice of ½ lime
1 tbsp soy sauce
2 tbsp sunflower oil
175g (6oz) baby corn, cut into 3 lengthways
1 small yellow pepper, deseeded and thinly sliced
2 pak choi, sliced into chunks
1 onion, finely sliced
2 tbsp freshly chopped Thai basil leaves

For the Thai-style sauce

2 tsp finely grated fresh root ginger
1 tbsp red Thai paste
1 x 160ml carton coconut cream
1 tbsp sweet chilli sauce
2 tbsp soy sauce
1 tsp light muscovado sugar
2 tsp cornflour

1. Measure all the ingredients for the Thai-style sauce into a bowl and mix well.
2. Place the steak strips in a bowl. Add the chilli, lime juice and soy sauce. Mix to coat and leave to marinate for about 30 minutes.
3. Heat 1 tablespoon of the oil in a non-stick frying pan over a high heat. Remove the beef from its marinade using a slotted spoon and add to the pan. Fry for a few minutes until golden brown. Remove from the pan and set aside.
4. Add the remaining oil to the pan, then add the baby corn, pepper, pak choi and onion and fry over a high heat for about 3 minutes, stirring occasionally. Pour in the Thai-style sauce and reserved marinade, stirring for 2 minutes until thickened.
5. Return the beef to the pan and season with salt and freshly ground black pepper. Sprinkle with basil to serve.

MARY'S TIPS

Best made and served. Beef can be marinated up to 2 hours ahead.

Not suitable for freezing.

Swiss Herb Beef and Potato Gratin

A mince ragu with a layered potato topping – a perfect family supper dish for all ages. Best to use small courgettes as large ones release too much water and make the dish sloppy.

Serves 6–8

3 tbsp sunflower oil
2 onions, diced
1kg (2lb 4oz) minced beef
2 fat garlic cloves, finely grated
2 tbsp tomato purée
2 × 400g tins chopped tomatoes
1 tsp caster sugar

For the topping

750g (1lb 10oz) small courgettes, sliced into 1cm (½in) rounds
3 large potatoes, cut into 2cm (¾in) dice
300g (10½oz) full-fat cream cheese
1 tbsp freshly chopped parsley
1 garlic clove, finely grated
1 tbsp snipped chives
1 tbsp cornflour
1 generous tbsp pouring double cream
115g (4oz) Parmesan, coarsely grated

MARY'S TIPS

Can be made and assembled up to 8 hours ahead.

Mince ragu freezes well before topping.

1. You will need a 2.25 litre (4 pint) wide-based ovenproof dish. Preheat the oven to 160°C/Fan 140°C/Gas 3.
2. Heat 2 tablespoons of the oil in a large flameproof casserole over a high heat. Add the onions and fry for a few minutes. Add the mince and brown all over. Add the garlic and fry for 30 seconds. Stir in the tomato purée and chopped tomatoes, and season generously with salt and freshly ground black pepper. Bring up to the boil, cover with a lid and transfer to the oven for 45–60 minutes, or until the mince is tender.
3. Check the seasoning and add the sugar, if the tomatoes are sharp. Spoon into the wide-based ovenproof dish and level the surface. Increase the oven temperature to 220°C/Fan 200°C/Gas 7.
4. Heat the remaining oil in a large frying pan over a medium heat. Add the courgettes and fry in batches until golden on both sides but not too soft. Remove from the pan with a slotted spoon and drain on kitchen paper. Arrange the courgettes in a layer over the top of the mince.
5. Meanwhile, boil the potatoes in boiling salted water for 3–5 minutes, until they are just cooked, then drain.
6. Spoon the cream cheese, parsley, garlic, chives, cornflour and double cream into a bowl and mix using an electric handwhisk until the cream cheese is smooth. Add the warm potatoes to the cheese mixture, then gently fold them in. The warm potatoes will loosen the cheese mixture. Spoon the potato mixture on top of the courgettes, then sprinkle with the Parmesan. Bake in the oven for about 35 minutes, or until bubbling and golden on top.

Scrumpy Beef Casserole with Parsley and Horseradish Dumplings

Just a little bit different and packed with flavour, these dumplings were an experiment that worked well. I patted out the suet dough to a rectangle, spread it with a mixture of parsley and horseradish, then rolled it up like a Swiss roll, sliced it and put it on top of the stew: a sort of savoury, Chelsea bun-dumpling! All so simple and can be prepared well ahead.

Serves 6–8

2 tbsp olive oil
1kg (2lb 4oz) braising steak, cut into 3cm(1¼in) cubes
1 onion, sliced
2 carrots, cut diagonally into 5mm (¼in) slices
2 celery sticks, cut into 5mm (¼in) slices
25g (1oz) plain flour
500ml (18fl oz) strong dry cider
1 beef stock cube
Small bunch of thyme
1 bay leaf
150g (5oz) button mushrooms, halved
1 tbsp Worcestershire sauce
Dash of gravy browning

For the dumplings

175g (6oz) self-raising flour
75g (3oz) shredded suet
½ tsp salt
½ tsp freshly ground black pepper

1. Preheat the oven to 150°C/Fan 130°C/Gas 2.
2. Heat 1 tablespoon of the oil in a large, deep flameproof casserole or ovenproof frying pan that has a lid over a high heat. Brown the meat all over (you may need to do this in batches), then remove with a slotted spoon and set aside.
3. Add the remaining oil, the onion, carrots and celery to the pan, and fry for about 5 minutes.
4. Meanwhile, measure the flour into a bowl, mix with a little of the cider and stir to make a smooth paste. Add the remaining cider to the bowl and whisk until smooth. Pour this cider mixture into the pan, and stir. Finally, add the stock cube, thyme and bay leaf, and bring to the boil. Return the beef to the pan, season with salt and freshly ground black pepper, cover with a lid and transfer to the preheated oven for about 1 hour 45 minutes, or until the beef is tender.
5. Add the mushrooms, Worcestershire sauce and gravy browning to the casserole, then return to the oven for 15 minutes.
6. Meanwhile, prepare the dumplings. Mix together the flour, suet, salt and pepper in a bowl. Stir in enough water to bring them together in a soft but not sticky dough. Turn out on to a lightly floured work surface and pat or roll out to a 15 x 20cm (6 x 8in) rectangle.

- 10 tbsp cold water (approximately)
- 3 tbsp very hot horseradish sauce
- 3 tbsp freshly chopped parsley

7. Place the horseradish and parsley in a small bowl and stir together with a little salt and pepper to form a paste. Spread this evenly over the surface of the dough, right up to the edges. Roll up the dough from one short end, Swiss-roll style, then cover with clingfilm and keep in the fridge until ready to use.
8. After 2 hours, remove the casserole from the oven, and increase the temperature to 200°C/Fan 180°C/Gas 6.
9. Remove the dumpling roll from the fridge and cut evenly into 8 rounds. Arrange these cut-side up on top of the casserole, sitting in the juices. Bring up to simmering point over a direct heat, then return to the oven to bake for 30 minutes, or until the dumplings start to get a golden crust. Serve immediately.

MARY'S TIPS

Prepare and cook the casserole for 2 hours, then cool quickly, cover and put in the fridge. Prepare the dumplings as far as forming the dough into a roll, cover closely with clingfilm and put in the fridge.

Both items can be kept for up to 2 days, or in the freezer for 6 months.

Reheat the casserole over a direct heat, then drop in the dumplings and bake as the recipe.

Cottage Pie with Crushed Potato Topping

This classic recipe uses crushed potatoes as a topping, instead of the standard mash, to make a nice change.

Serves 6–8

1 tbsp sunflower oil
2 large onions, chopped
4 celery sticks, finely diced
1kg (2lb 4oz) lean minced beef
55g (2oz) plain flour
300ml (½ pint) red wine
300ml (½ pint) beef stock
1 tbsp Worcestershire sauce
1 tbsp redcurrant jelly
1 tbsp freshly chopped thyme
Dash of gravy browning

For the topping

1kg (2lb) new potatoes, unpeeled and scrubbed
3 tbsp olive oil
1 large garlic clove, finely grated
55g (2oz) Parmesan, finely grated

1. You will need a shallow 2 litre (3½ pint) ovenproof dish. Preheat the oven to 160°C/Fan 140°C/Gas 3.

2. Heat the oil in a deep, ovenproof frying pan or saucepan, add the onions and celery and fry over a high heat for 3–4 minutes. Add the mince and brown all over for about 5 minutes, stirring and breaking up the meat with a wooden spoon until no pink remains.

3. Sprinkle in the flour and fry, stirring for a minute. Add the remaining ingredients and season with salt and freshly ground black pepper. Bring to the boil, cover with a lid and transfer to the oven to cook for about 1½ hours, or until tender.

4. Meanwhile, place the potatoes in a saucepan of salted water, bring to the boil and boil for 15–20 minutes until just tender. Drain, return to the pan and, using a fork, break the potatoes into large rough chunks. Drizzle in the olive oil, add the garlic and season. Toss to coat well, then set aside.

5. When the meat is cooked, remove from the oven and increase the temperature to 200°C/Fan 180°C/Gas 6. Transfer the cooked mince to the ovenproof dish and spoon over the crushed potatoes. Sprinkle with the Parmesan, then bake in the preheated oven for 30–40 minutes, or until bubbling and golden-tinged on top.

MARY'S TIPS

The assembled dish can be prepared up to a day ahead and kept in the fridge. Once cooked, it can be stored in the fridge for 1–2 days.

The mince is best frozen without the topping. Defrost the meat and top with fresh potato as required.

Mexican Tortilla Bake

This all-in-one dish is so quick to make. Think of a Mexican-inspired lasagne using ready-made tortillas instead of sheets of pasta. This was an idea from my friend and assistant, Lucy Young, and is now a regular bake for all of us. Utterly delicious and very moreish!

Serves 6

For the mince

1 tbsp olive oil

2 large onions, roughly chopped

500g (1 lb 2oz) lean minced beef

1 mild red chilli, deseeded and finely chopped

1 red pepper, deseeded and diced

2 garlic cloves, crushed

1 tbsp ground cumin

1 tbsp ground coriander

2 tbsp tomato purée

1–2 tbsp mango chutney

2 × 400g tins chopped tomatoes

Small bunch of coriander, leaves chopped

To assemble

3 large tortilla wraps

250g (9oz) full-fat mascarpone

115g (4oz) mozzarella, grated

115g (4oz) Cheddar, grated

1. You will need a 1.5 litre (2½pint) wide-based, shallow ovenproof dish. Preheat the oven to 180°C/Fan 160°C/Gas 4.
2. Pour the oil into a large ovenproof frying pan over a medium heat, add the onions and fry for 3 minutes. Turn up the heat, tip in the minced beef and fry until brown, breaking up the meat with a wooden spoon and stirring occasionally. Add the chilli, red pepper, garlic and spices, and fry for about 5 minutes until all the mixture is quite dry. Stir in the tomato purée, mango chutney and tinned tomatoes, and season well with salt and freshly ground black pepper. Cover with a lid, bring to the boil and transfer to the oven to simmer for 1 hour.
3. Remove from the oven and stir in half the coriander. Increase the oven temperature to 200°C/Fan 180°C/Gas 6.
4. Spread a third of the beef mixture over the bottom of the ovenproof dish and lay one tortilla wrap on top. Spread a third of the mascarpone (see tip) over the tortilla and sprinkle with a third of each of the mozzarella and Cheddar. Repeat twice more so you have three layers.
5. Bake in the oven for about 25–30 minutes until golden and bubbling. Set aside for 5 minutes before serving scattered with the remaining coriander.

MARY'S TIPS

If the mascarpone is firm, spread it on each tortilla before adding to the dish.

The dish can be assembled up to 6 hours ahead, then baked to serve. Freezes well uncooked.

Beef and Ale Casserole with Pickled Walnuts

A rich and delicious casserole – perfect to have in the freezer for last-minute guests.

Serves 6

- 3 tbsp sunflower oil
- 800g (1¾lb) braising beef, cut into 3cm (1¼in) cubes
- 3 large onions, sliced
- 2 carrots, diced
- 3 celery sticks, sliced
- 2 large garlic cloves, grated
- 55g (2oz) plain flour
- 500ml (18fl oz) ale
- 200ml (⅓ pint) beef stock
- 3 bay leaves
- 2 tbsp redcurrant jelly
- 1 × 390g jar pickled walnuts, drained and quartered

1. Preheat the oven to 150°C/Fan 130°C/Gas 2.
2. Heat the oil in a large ovenproof frying pan that has a lid or a flameproof casserole over a medium heat. Season the beef with salt and freshly ground black pepper, then add to the pan and fry until brown (you may need to do this in batches). Using a slotted spoon, transfer the beef to a plate and set aside.
3. Add the onions to the pan and fry for a few minutes, then add the carrots, celery and garlic and fry for 3 minutes. Return the beef to the pan.
4. Meanwhile, measure the flour into a bowl and add a small amount of the ale. Whisk until you have a smooth paste. Pour in the remining ale, whisking all the time. Pour the ale mixture and stock into the pan and bring up to the boil. Stir in the bay leaves, redcurrant jelly and lots of seasoning. Cover with a lid and transfer to the preheated oven for 2 hours.
5. Add the pickled walnuts and continue to cook for another 30 minutes until tender.

MARY'S TIPS

Prepare and cook the casserole for 2 hours, then cool quickly, cover and put in the fridge. It will keep for up to 2 days. Reheat over a direct heat, add the walnuts and cook for 30 minutes to serve.

Freezes well without the walnuts.

Lamb Tagine

I have travelled to Morocco where tagines, like this, are a staple dish. This is my quick version, as some tagines take three hours to cook. The spices used here are a classic combination and give a wonderful depth of flavour.

Serves 6

- 2–3 tbsp sunflower oil
- 750g (1lb 10oz) lamb neck fillet, sliced into 2–3cm (¾–1¼in) pieces
- 2 large onions, sliced
- 3 celery sticks, sliced
- 2 garlic cloves, finely grated
- 4cm (1½in) piece of fresh root ginger, peeled and grated
- 1 tbsp ground cumin
- 1 tbsp ground coriander
- 2 tsp ground cinnamon
- 1 × 400g tin chopped tomatoes
- 450ml (¾ pint) chicken or lamb stock
- 2 tbsp tomato purée
- 2 tsp harissa paste
- 1 tbsp runny honey
- 8 ready-to-eat dried apricots, quartered
- 2 preserved lemons, each sliced into 8 pieces and any pips removed (see tip)
- 1 × 400g tin chickpeas, drained and rinsed
- 2 tbsp freshly chopped parsley

1. Preheat the oven to 150°C/Fan 130°C/Gas 2.
2. Heat the oil in a deep ovenproof frying pan that has a lid, or a large flameproof casserole over a high heat. Season the lamb with salt and freshly ground black pepper, then add to the pan and fry for 3–4 minutes or until golden brown all over. You may need to do this in batches. Use a slotted spoon to transfer the meat to a plate.
3. Add the onions and celery to the pan and fry over a medium heat for 3–4 minutes until starting to soften but not browned. Add the garlic and ginger, then sprinkle in the spices and stir to coat the vegetables. Cook for 10 seconds, then add the tomatoes, stock, tomato purée, harissa paste, honey, apricots and preserved lemons. Bring to the boil, stirring, then return the lamb and any juices to the pan. Season with salt and freshly ground black pepper, cover with the lid and transfer to the oven to cook for 1 hour.
4. Remove from the oven, stir in the chickpeas and check the seasoning. Return to the oven, uncovered, to cook for another ½–1 hour, or until the onions have softened and the meat is tender.
5. Sprinkle with the chopped parsley to serve.

MARY'S TIPS

Preserved lemons are available to buy in the specialist ingredient selection of good supermarkets.

Can be made up to 1 day ahead and reheated. The cooked dish freezes well.

Sweet Smoked Paprika Lamb with Borlotti Beans

Cooked in one pot, this makes a great dish for a family gathering. If you want to make a more generous serving, simply add another tin of borlotti beans. You'll need to buy sliced chorizo, rather than chunky cubes, for this recipe.

Serves 6–8

2 tbsp sunflower oil
1kg (2lb 4oz) diced lamb (from a leg of lamb)
175g (6oz) sliced chorizo, cut into small pieces
2 red onions, sliced
2 garlic cloves, finely grated
1 aubergine, cut into 4cm (1½in) cubes
2 tsp sweet smoked paprika (see tip)
150ml (¼ pint) white wine
2 × 400g tins chopped tomatoes
1 tbsp light muscovado sugar
1 × 400g tin borlotti beans, drained and rinsed
Handful of freshly chopped parsley (optional)

1. Preheat the oven to 160°C/Fan 140°C/Gas 3.
2. Heat the oil in a large, deep ovenproof frying pan that has a lid or a flameproof casserole over a high heat. Add the lamb and fry until browned – you will need to do this in batches. Remove the meat with a slotted spoon, place on a plate and set aside.
3. Add the chorizo to the pan and cook until browned and crisp, then remove with a slotted spoon and add to the lamb.
4. Tip in the onions and garlic and fry for about 3–4 minutes. Add the aubergine and fry for another 2 minutes. Sprinkle in the paprika and fry for a further 2 minutes. Pour in the wine and tomatoes, and add the sugar. Return the browned lamb and chorizo to the pan, season with salt and freshly ground black pepper and bring to the boil, stirring. Cover the pan with a lid and transfer to the oven to cook for 1 hour.
5. Remove the dish from the oven and stir in the drained beans. Bring back up to the boil on the hob, cover again and return to the oven for a further 30 minutes, or until the lamb is tender.
6. Sprinkle with chopped parsley, if using, and serve immediately.

MARY'S TIPS

It's important to use sweet smoked paprika, rather than hot smoked, which is more like chilli and will make the dish very hot!

The lamb can be cooked up to 2 days ahead, the beans added when reheating. Freezes well.

Minted Lamb Casserole with Porcini Mushrooms

A casserole full of flavour and perfect for preparing ahead – one of my favourite lamb casseroles.

Serves 6

30g (1oz) dried porcini mushrooms
150ml (¼ pint) boiling water
2 tbsp olive oil
900g (2lb) lamb neck fillet, cubed
1 large onion, sliced
2 garlic cloves, finely grated
25g (1oz) plain flour
300ml (½ pint) red wine
150ml (¼ pint) chicken stock
1 tbsp Worcestershire sauce
2 tbsp mint jelly
250g (9oz) brown chestnut mushrooms, halved

1. Preheat the oven to 160°C/Fan 140°C/Gas 3.
2. Place the mushrooms in a small bowl, pour over the boiling water and leave to soak for 30 minutes. Strain through a sieve, reserving the liquid, and chop the mushrooms fairly finely.
3. Heat 1 tablespoon of the oil in an ovenproof frying pan that has a lid, or a flameproof casserole. Season the lamb with salt and freshly ground black pepper, then add to the pan and fry until golden and sealed all over – you may need to do this in batches. Remove with a slotted spoon and set aside.
4. Heat the remaining oil in the pan, add the onion and garlic, and fry for a few minutes.
5. Measure the flour into a small bowl, whisk in a little red wine until smooth and blended, then pour in the remaining wine. Add this mixture to the pan followed by the stock, Worcestershire sauce, mint jelly, chopped soaked mushrooms and reserved mushroom liquid. Stir and bring to the boil.
6. Return the lamb to the pan, cover and cook in the oven for 1½ hours or until the lamb is tender. Add the chestnut mushrooms 15 minutes before the end of cooking.

MARY'S TIPS

The casserole can be made up to 1 day ahead and reheated.

It freezes well, cooked without the mushrooms. Add the mushrooms when reheating, to serve.

French Slow-roast Lamb with Ratatouille

This all-in-one slow roast with ratatouille-style vegetables is great for feeding a crowd. It does need a long time in the oven, but this means that the lamb is beautifully tender and you have time to pop to the pub or go for a walk!

Serves 6

Large leg or shoulder of lamb (about 2kg/4lb 7oz), bone in

2 garlic cloves, sliced into slivers

3 onions, thickly sliced

1 × 400g tin chopped tomatoes

300ml (½ pint) beef or chicken stock

2 tbsp sun-dried tomato paste

1 tbsp freshly chopped thyme

3 fresh bay leaves

1 tbsp honey

2 red peppers, deseeded and chopped into large pieces

1 large aubergine, chopped into large pieces

2 tsp paprika

For the rub

2 tbsp freshly chopped thyme

1 tbsp paprika

2 tbsp olive oil

1. Preheat the oven to 220°C/Fan 200°C/Gas 7.
2. For the rub, put the thyme, paprika and oil in a small bowl, season with salt and freshly ground black pepper, and mix well.
3. Make holes in the lamb joint with a small, sharp knife and spread the rub all over it. Insert the garlic slivers into the holes and put the lamb in a large, deep roasting tin. Add the onions around and underneath. Roast in the preheated oven for about 40 minutes.
4. Meanwhile, pour the tomatoes into a bowl, add the stock, sun-dried tomato paste, thyme, bay leaves and honey, and stir to combine.
5. Remove the tin from the oven and lower the oven temperature to 160°C/Fan 140°C/Gas 3. Scatter the peppers and aubergine pieces around the lamb, and pour the tomato mixture into the roasting tin, over the peppers and aubergine, and stir. Sprinkle the paprika over the vegetables, then cover the whole tin with foil. Roast in the oven for about 4 hours, or until the lamb is tender and falling off the bone.
6. Shred the meat or carve into slices. Drain any fat from the top of the sauce and serve the meat with the ratatouille vegetables alongside.

MARY'S TIPS

Best made to serve but the lamb and ratatouille will keep for up to 4 hours in the fridge before roasting. Not suitable for freezing.

Veggie Mains

Orzo with Broad Beans, Peas, Lemon and Thyme

Aubergine Caponata

Baked Macaroni Cheese with Tomatoes

Roasted Romano Peppers with Puy Lentils and Feta

Paneer and Roasted Vegetable Curry

Leek and Stilton Tart

Mushroom and Asparagus Risotto

Vegetable Pad Thai

Garlic Mushroom Penne Gratin

Mixed Bean and Red Pepper Chilli

Humble Pie

Super Veg with Brown Rice and Herbs

Shakshuka

Lentil Shepherd's Pie

Frittata with Spinach, Feta and Tomatoes

Orzo with Broad Beans, Peas, Lemon and Thyme

Orzo is a type of pasta made in the shape of a large grain of rice. It's a bit different yet very versatile – I find I use it more and more. It can be served on its own or used in a range of dishes, from soups and salads to casseroles. The recipe I've included here is rather like a risotto. Orzo grains remain more separate than risotto rice, but the finished dish is just as creamy and tasty. It's also much quicker to prepare, making it perfect for an everyday lunch or supper.

Serves 4

200g (7oz) dried orzo
200g (7oz) frozen baby broad beans, defrosted and outer skin removed
200g (7oz) frozen petits pois, defrosted
Knob of butter
1 tbsp olive oil
1 onion, very thinly sliced
2 garlic cloves, finely grated
200g (7oz) full-fat crème fraîche
1 tbsp freshly chopped thyme
Finely grated zest and juice of 1 lemon
25g (1oz) Parmesan, coarsely grated

To serve
25g (1oz) pine nuts, toasted (see tip)
25g (1oz) Parmesan, coarsely grated

1. Cook the orzo in boiling salted water according to the packet instructions (usually about 10 minutes), or until just cooked (see tip), then drain. Boil the broad beans and petits pois in a separate pan for 2–3 minutes, then drain and rinse.

2. Meanwhile, heat the butter and oil in a large frying pan over a high heat. When the butter has melted, add the onion and fry for 2–3 minutes. Cover with a lid, then reduce the heat and cook gently for about 15 minutes, or until soft. Add the garlic, turn up the heat and fry for 1 minute.

3. Stir in the crème fraîche, then add the cooked orzo, beans and peas, and gently heat together. Add the thyme, lemon zest and juice and Parmesan, stir together and season to taste with salt and freshly ground black pepper.

4. Spoon into a serving dish and scatter with the pine nuts and grated Parmesan to serve.

MARY'S TIPS

Don't overcook the pasta as it will absorb the cream on standing and it shouldn't be too stodgy.

Toast the pine nuts in a dry pan over a medium heat for 4–5 minutes, tossing frequently to ensure they don't burn. You could use ready-toasted pine nuts otherwise.

Not suitable for freezing.

Aubergine Caponata

Traditionally made with green olives and red wine vinegar, I prefer using soft black pitted olives and white wine vinegar, as I always have them in the cupboard.

Serves 4

8 tbsp olive oil
2 aubergines, cut into 2cm (¾in) cubes
2 onions, finely chopped
2 celery sticks, finely chopped
1 red pepper, deseeded and cut into 1cm (½in) cubes
3 large garlic cloves, finely grated
500g (1lb 2oz) passata
115g (4oz) soft pitted black olives
2 tbsp white wine vinegar
3 tbsp capers from a jar, drained
1½ tbsp caster sugar
3 tbsp freshly chopped parsley

1. Heat 3 tablespoons of the oil in a large frying pan that has a lid over a high heat. Add half of the aubergine and fry until browned. Remove the aubergine from the pan and set aside. Heat another 3 tablespoons of the oil in the pan and fry the remaining aubergine. Set aside with the rest.

2. Heat the remaining oil in the pan. Add the onions, celery and pepper and fry over a high heat for 3–4 minutes. Add the garlic and fry for a few seconds. Return the aubergine to the pan, add the passata, olives, vinegar, capers and sugar. Season with salt and freshly ground black pepper, cover with a lid and bring up to the boil. Reduce the heat and simmer gently for 20–25 minutes.

3. Remove the lid from the pan and simmer for another 5 minutes, until the sauce has reduced and the vegetables are soft but not mushy.

4. Sprinkle with parsley and serve with crusty bread, couscous or as a vegetable side dish.

MARY'S TIP

Can be made up to a day ahead and reheated to serve.

Freezes for up to a month.

Baked Macaroni Cheese with Tomatoes

This is one for the children, though secretly all the grown-ups love it too!

Serves 6

275g (10oz) macaroni
55g (2oz) butter
55g (2oz) plain flour
1 litre (1¾ pints) hot milk (see tip)
1½ tsp Dijon mustard
150g (5oz) extra-mature Cheddar, grated
4 large tomatoes, halved and sliced

1. You will need a 1.75 litre (3 pint) ovenproof dish. Preheat the oven to 200°C/Fan 180°C/Gas 6.
2. Bring a pan of salted water to the boil, add the macaroni and cook according to the packet instructions or until al dente (just undercooked). Drain and refresh in cold water.
3. To make the cheese sauce, melt the butter in a saucepan, add the flour and whisk over a high heat for 30 seconds. Gradually whisk in the hot milk over a high heat, then bring to the boil and cook for 2 minutes until thickened and smooth.
4. Remove from the heat, add the mustard and two-thirds of the cheese and season well with salt and freshly ground black pepper.
5. Add the cooked macaroni to the sauce, stir to combine, then pour into the ovenproof dish. Arrange the tomato slices, slightly overlapping, on top and push down slightly into the sauce. Sprinkle with the remaining cheese. Bake in the oven for 25–30 minutes until golden, piping hot and bubbling.
6. Serve straight from the oven.

MARY'S TIP

Adding hot milk enables the roux (butter and flour mixture) to absorb the milk quickly and the sauce to come to the boil more rapidly, making it less likely to be lumpy. Semi-skimmed or full-fat milk doesn't matter – use whatever you have in the fridge.

Can be assembled up to 12 hours ahead.

Freezes well without the tomatoes.

Roasted Romano Peppers with Puy Lentils and Feta

These are wonderful as a main dish for vegetarians or as a side dish for a buffet or BBQ. Romano peppers are long, mild red peppers.

Serves 4–6

115g (4oz) dried Puy lentils
2 large garlic cloves, finely grated
2 tbsp balsamic vinegar
3 tbsp sun-dried tomato paste
1 tbsp freshly chopped thyme
4 tbsp freshly chopped parsley, plus extra to garnish
4 spring onions, sliced
8 peppadew peppers, chopped
115g (4oz) cherry tomatoes, quartered
150g (5oz) feta, crumbled
3 large Romano peppers
2 tbsp olive oil, plus extra for greasing

1. Preheat the oven to 200°C/Fan 180°C/Gas 6 and grease a roasting tin.
2. Cook the lentils in boiling water according to the packet instructions. Drain and tip into a bowl.
3. Add the garlic, vinegar, sun-dried tomato paste, herbs, spring onions, peppadew peppers, tomatoes and 115g (4oz) of the feta to the lentils. Season well with black pepper and mix well.
4. Slice the peppers in half lengthways through the stem, keeping them intact, and remove the seeds. Divide the lentil filling between the pepper halves and place in the prepared tin. Sprinkle the remaining feta over the top and drizzle with the oil. Roast in the oven for about 25 minutes, or until the feta is tinged brown and the peppers are soft but still holding their shape.
5. Scatter with parsley to serve, if using.

MARY'S TIPS

Can be assembled up to 6 hours ahead and cooked to serve.

Not for freezing.

Paneer and Roasted Vegetable Curry

Paneer is a fresh Indian cheese that does not have a strong flavour but stays firm when roasted. It combines beautifully with the vegetables in this delicious curry. Lovely served with some naan bread.

Serves 4–6

4 tbsp sunflower oil
1 small cauliflower, broken into florets
300g (10½oz) sweet potato, peeled and cut into 2cm (¾in) dice
225g (8oz) paneer, cut into 2cm (¾in) dice
2 large onions, sliced
3cm (1¼in) piece of fresh root ginger, peeled and grated
1 tbsp curry powder
1 tbsp garam masala
¼ tsp ground cloves
2 tbsp plain flour
600ml (1 pint) hot vegetable stock
2 tbsp mango chutney
150ml (¼ pint) pouring double cream
100g (3½oz) baby spinach
Juice of ½–1 lemon

1. Preheat the oven to 220°C/Fan 200°C/Gas 7.
2. Drizzle 2 tablespoons of the oil into a large roasting tin. Scatter the pieces of cauliflower and sweet potato into the tin and toss to coat them with oil. Season with salt and pepper.
3. Roast in the oven for about 15 minutes. Add the paneer at one end of the hot roasting tin and return it to the oven. Cook for 5–10 minutes, turning halfway through, until the cheese is golden on both sides, the cauliflower is golden and the sweet potato is tender. Set aside.
4. Heat the remaining oil in a large, deep frying pan. Add the onions and ginger and fry for 5–10 minutes until cooked. Sprinkle in the spices and flour and stir over the heat for a few seconds. Gradually pour in the stock and stir until thickened, then simmer for a few minutes over a high heat.
5. Stir in the mango chutney and cream, then add the roasted cauliflower and sweet potato to the pan. Stir in the spinach until it has heated through and wilted, then add the lemon juice and check the seasoning.
6. Add the paneer at the last moment and serve piping hot.

MARY'S TIPS

Best made and served.

Not suitable for freezing.

Leek and Stilton Tart

Whether called a quiche or a tart, it's all the same, and all with a thin layer of pastry and an abundant filling. Although it looks like a long cooking time, this can be prepared in easy stages; cooking the base first and leaving to cool, then filling later.

Serves 6–8

For the pastry

225g (8oz) plain flour, plus extra for dusting

125g (4½oz) cold butter, cubed, plus extra for greasing

1 egg, beaten with ½ tbsp water

For the filling

1 tbsp olive oil

2 leeks, thinly sliced

2 celery sticks, thinly sliced

4 eggs

400ml (14fl oz) pouring double cream

150g (5oz) Stilton, coarsely grated

2 tbsp freshly chopped parsley

MARY'S TIPS

Can be made up to 8 hours ahead and reheated. The pastry base can be cooked a day ahead.

Both the cooked tart and the unfilled pastry base freeze well.

1. You will need a 28cm (11in) round, loose-bottomed deep tart tin, preferably fluted. Grease the tin with butter.
2. To make the pastry, measure the flour and butter into a food processor and whiz until the mixture resembles breadcrumbs. Add the egg and whiz into a smooth ball of dough. Alternatively, rub the flour and butter together in a mixing bowl with your fingertips before adding the egg.
3. Roll the pastry out on a lightly floured work surface to a disc slightly larger than the tin and about the thickness of a £1 coin. Carefully transfer the pastry to the tin, pressing it into the base and sides. Form a little lip around the edge of the tin, trim off any excess pastry and prick the base with a fork. Place in the fridge to chill for about 15 minutes. Preheat the oven to 200°C/Fan 180°C/Gas 6.
4. Line the pastry case with non-stick baking paper and baking beans, and bake blind in the preheated oven for 15 minutes. Remove the beans and paper and return to the oven for a further 5–10 minutes, or until just cooked and pale golden. Reduce the oven temperature to 180°C/Fan 160°C/Gas 4.
5. Meanwhile, make the filling. Heat the oil in a frying pan over a high heat. Add the leeks and celery and fry for 2–3 minutes. Reduce the heat to low, cover with a lid and cook for 20–25 minutes, or until the vegetables are completely tender. Remove the lid, increase the heat and fry for another minute to drive off any excess liquid. Remove the pan from the heat.
6. Beat the eggs and cream together in a jug and season with salt and pepper.

7. Spoon the cooked leeks and celery into the baked pastry case, then scatter with the cheese and parsley. Season with salt and pepper, and pour the egg and cream mixture over the top.
8. Bake in the oven for about 35–40 minutes, or until golden brown and just set on top. Leave for 5–10 minutes to rest before turning out.

Mushroom and Asparagus Risotto

My quick risotto is full of flavour from all the fresh ingredients. An oven-baked risotto is a good alternative – prepare as here but add all the stock at once and pop into the oven, preheated to 200°C/Fan 180°C/Gas 6, to cook for around 20 minutes. Stir in the vegetables 3 minutes before the end, then finish off with the cheese, butter and chives before serving.

Serves 4–6

1 tbsp sunflower oil
1 large onion, finely chopped
1 large garlic clove, finely grated
275g (10oz) risotto rice
100ml (3½fl oz) white wine
150g (5oz) asparagus spears, stalks sliced into rounds and tips reserved
About 800ml (28fl oz) hot chicken or vegetable stock
350g (12oz) mixed button and chestnut mushrooms, sliced
75g (3oz) Parmesan, grated
1 bunch of chives, snipped
Knob of butter

1. Heat the oil in a wide-based shallow saucepan (see tip) over a high heat. Add the onion and garlic and fry for a few minutes. Add the rice and stir to coat the grains. Pour in the wine and boil for a few minutes until nearly evaporated. Toss in the sliced asparagus stalks and add the hot stock, a ladleful at a time, stirring over the high heat, until all the stock has been absorbed, and the rice is just tender. Make sure that each spoonful of stock is absorbed before adding the next. It should take around 20 minutes to cook, from when the stock is added.
2. Add the mushrooms and the asparagus tips to the pan, and stir for about 3 minutes, until well combined with the rice and just softened.
3. Remove from the heat. Add the Parmesan, chives and butter, and season to taste with salt and freshly ground black pepper. Stir and cover with a lid. Leave to stand for 2 minutes before serving.

MARY'S TIPS

Use a wide-based pan so the liquid evaporates quickly.

Best made and served immediately, though any leftovers can be chilled and made into cakes to fry and enjoy the following day.

Not suitable for freezing.

Vegetable Pad Thai

Commonly served as street food in Thailand, this noodle dish is very popular in the West, too. Tamarind paste is a sweet and sour paste made from the tamarind fruit. It is more traditional to serve this without the omelette. Or you could fry an egg and serve that on top of each portion, if you wish.

Serves 6

3 tbsp sunflower oil
3 eggs, beaten
200g (7oz) flat rice noodles
1 large carrot, cut into matchsticks
1 red pepper, deseeded and thinly sliced
3 large banana shallots, sliced
½ red chilli, deseeded and finely chopped
Small bunch of coriander, roughly chopped
115g (4oz) beansprouts
75g (3oz) salted peanuts, chopped
1 lime, cut into wedges, to serve

For the sauce

2 tbsp soy sauce
3 tbsp fish sauce (or vegetarian alternative)
2 tbsp light muscovado sugar
2 tsp tamarind paste
3 garlic cloves, finely grated
2 tbsp sweet chilli sauce
Juice of 1 large lime

1. Mix all the sauce ingredients together in a small bowl and set aside.

2. Heat a large frying pan or wok over a medium-high heat. Add 1 tablespoon of the oil and the eggs and swirl them around the pan to make a thin, flat omelette. Cook for 2–3 minutes until set, then flip over and cook for another minute. Transfer to a board and slice into very thin strips.

3. Cook the noodles in boiling water according to the packet instructions. Drain and refresh under cold water. Drain again.

4. Heat the remaining oil in the large pan over a high heat. Add the carrot, pepper and shallots and fry for 4–5 minutes. Add the chilli and fry for 30 seconds. Add the cooked noodles and toss everything together.

5. Pour in the sauce, season with freshly ground black pepper and toss over the heat quickly until well mixed and heated through.

6. Add the coriander, beansprouts, peanuts and strips of omelette, and serve at once with a wedge of lime alongside.

MARY'S TIP

Prep the ingredients and cook to serve.

Not suitable for freezing.

Garlic Mushroom Penne Gratin

An all-in-one dish that can be made ahead and is perfect for serving the whole family. A mixture of field and chestnut mushrooms is given below, but you can use any mushrooms you like – closed or open cup, button, chestnut or oyster.

Serves 6

300g (10½oz) dried penne
25g (1oz) butter
1 onion, chopped
2 garlic cloves, finely grated
500g (1lb 2oz) mixed field and chestnut mushrooms, thickly sliced
200ml (⅓ pint) pouring double cream
55g (2oz) Parmesan, grated
2 tbsp snipped chives
75g (3oz) mature Cheddar, grated
Paprika, for dusting

1. You will need a shallow 2 litre (3½ pint) ovenproof dish.
2. Cook the pasta in boiling, salted water according to the packet instructions until just cooked. Drain and refresh in cold water to stop the pasta cooking further, then leave to drain again in the colander.
3. Melt the butter in a large frying pan over a high heat. Add the onion and fry for 4 minutes, then lower the heat, cover with a lid and cook for about 10 minutes until soft.
4. Remove the lid and turn up the heat, then add the garlic and mushrooms, and fry quickly for 3–4 minutes until the mushrooms are just cooked. Season with salt and freshly ground black pepper.
5. Tip the drained pasta into the pan, pour in the cream and toss together. Add the Parmesan and chives, check the seasoning and mix until combined.
6. Pour into the ovenproof dish and sprinkle with the Cheddar and paprika. Slide under a hot grill for about 5 minutes until golden and bubbling around the edges.
7. Serve immediately.

MARY'S TIP

The pasta can be cooked up to a day ahead, then kept in the fridge. If making ahead, add a little more cream to the sauce as the pasta will absorb some of the moisture when standing. The dish can be assembled fully and chilled overnight, then cooked at 200°C/Fan 180°C/Gas 6 for 30 minutes.

Mixed Bean and Red Pepper Chilli

Delicious for everyone, not just vegetarians, this healthy chilli is bursting with flavour. Serve it with guacamole to make it extra special, and soured cream, too, if liked.

Serves 6

2 tbsp olive oil
1 large onion, finely chopped
1 red pepper, deseeded and diced
2 garlic cloves, finely grated
1 tbsp ground cumin
1 tbsp ground coriander
1 tsp sweet smoked paprika
¼ tsp hot chilli powder
2 × 400g tins mixed salad beans, drained and rinsed
1 × 400g tin chopped tomatoes
500g (1lb 2oz) passata
300ml (½ pint) vegetable stock
1 tbsp tomato purée
1 tbsp mango chutney
1 × 198g tin sweetcorn, drained
Small bunch of coriander, leaves chopped

1. Heat the oil in a deep frying pan that has a lid over a high heat. Add the onion and pepper and fry for 3–4 minutes. Add the garlic and spices and fry for 10 seconds.
2. Stir in the beans, chopped tomatoes, passata, stock, tomato purée and mango chutney. Season with salt and freshly ground black pepper. Bring up to the boil, then reduce the heat, cover and simmer for about 40 minutes.
3. Check the seasoning and stir in the sweetcorn and coriander.
4. Serve the chilli with rice, grated cheese, soured cream and guacamole (see page 34), if liked.

MARY'S TIPS

Chilli can be made up to 8 hours ahead and reheated.

The chilli freezes well. Defrost and reheat on the hob to serve.

Humble Pie

Hearty, warming and a real treat! Using ready-rolled pastry makes this a very easy pie.

Serves 6

2 leeks, trimmed and cut into 2cm (¾in) slices
1 large cauliflower, broken into small florets and smaller leaves chopped
115g (4oz) frozen petits pois
Knob of butter
275g (10oz) button mushrooms, halved
1 × 320g packet ready-rolled puff pastry
1 egg, beaten

For the cheese sauce

55g (2oz) butter
55g (2oz) plain flour
450ml (¾ pint) hot milk
2 tsp Dijon mustard
115g (4oz) mature Cheddar, coarsely grated
55g (2oz) Parmesan, coarsely grated

1. You will need a deep 1.7 litre (3 pint) pie dish.
2. Bring a large pan of salted water to the boil. Add the leeks and boil for 4 minutes. Add the cauliflower florets and leaves, and boil for 3 minutes until just tender. Drain and run under cold water to stop the cooking. Drain again and set aside.
3. To make the cheese sauce, melt the butter in a large saucepan over a medium heat. Sprinkle in the flour and stir for 1 minute. Gradually add the hot milk, whisking until thickened. Stir in the mustard, Cheddar and Parmesan, and season well with salt and freshly ground black pepper. Leave to cool for 5 minutes.
4. Heat the butter in a frying pan over a high heat. Add the mushrooms and fry for 3 minutes until golden. Set aside to cool. Add all the cold vegetables and peas to the cheese sauce, stir and check the seasoning. Spoon into the pie dish, then set aside to cool. Preheat the oven to 200°C/Fan 180°C/Gas 6.
5. Unroll the pastry and remove a 7cm (2¾in) strip from one short side and chill in the fridge. Roll out the remaining pastry to slightly bigger than the top of the pie dish. Brush beaten egg around the edge of the dish, then place the pastry on top and press down to seal the edges. Trim any excess pastry with a sharp knife and make a small slit in the centre for the steam to escape. Brush the top with beaten egg.
6. Roll out the reserved strip of pastry to be a bit thinner, then roll it up tightly. Using a sharp knife, slice to make long, thin strips. Unravel and dip them into the egg wash, then arrange on top of the pie, in a random pattern. Bake in the preheated oven for about 40–45 minutes, until the pastry is golden and the sauce is bubbling around the edges.

MARY'S TIPS

The pie can be made, left unglazed and kept covered in the fridge up to 24 hours ahead.

Not suitable for freezing.

Super Veg with Brown Rice and Herbs

This is such a great dish to have as a regular part of your weekday meals. Lucy cooks it often and it can be served on its own in a bowl or with a grilled chicken breast. It's also good served cold as a rice salad.

Serves 4–6

200g (7oz) brown long-grain rice
1 tbsp sunflower oil
55g (2oz) butter
1 onion, chopped
1 fennel bulb, core removed, thinly sliced
175g (6oz) butternut squash, peeled and diced into small cubes (prepared weight)
1 garlic clove, finely grated
150ml (¼ pint) white wine
2 small courgettes, diced
200g (7oz) chestnut mushrooms, thinly sliced
Squeeze of lemon juice
3 tbsp freshly chopped parsley
1 tbsp freshly chopped thyme
2 tbsp toasted pumpkin seeds

1. Cook the rice in boiling water according to the packet instructions. Drain and set aside.
2. Heat the oil and butter in a large frying pan over a high heat. Add the onion, fennel and squash, and fry for 5 minutes. Add the garlic and fry for 10 seconds. Pour in the wine, cover the pan and simmer for 5 minutes until the squash is tender. Add the courgettes and mushrooms and fry for a few more minutes.
3. Toss in the cooked rice and lemon juice, and stir over the heat until the rice is heated through.
4. Add the herbs and season with salt and freshly ground black pepper. Serve sprinkled with the pumpkin seeds.

MARY'S TIPS

Can be made up to 8 hours ahead and served cold.

Not suitable for freezing.

Shakshuka

A popular Middle Eastern and North African dish, this can now be found on many breakfast menus. The name means 'mix up' in Arabic. It has a spiced tomato base with eggs on top and is such a quick and easy dish to make from storecupboard ingredients. There are many variations and additions to this historic recipe; some add aubergine, feta or spicy sausage.

Serves 4

2 tbsp olive oil
2 onions, roughly chopped
2 garlic cloves, finely grated
1 red chilli, deseeded and finely diced
2 × 400g tins chopped tomatoes
1 heaped tbsp sun-dried tomato paste
Pinch of caster sugar
4 eggs
2 tbsp freshly chopped parsley

1. Heat the oil in a deep frying pan that has a lid over a medium-high heat. Add the onions and fry for 5 minutes. Add the garlic and chilli and fry for 30 seconds. Stir in the chopped tomatoes, sun-dried tomato paste and sugar, and bring up to the boil. Reduce the heat and simmer gently, without a lid, for about 10 minutes, until the sauce has reduced and thickened and the onion is tender. Season well with salt and freshly ground black pepper.
2. Using the back of a spoon, make four dips in the sauce and carefully crack an egg into each one. Cover the pan with a lid and simmer over a gentle heat for about 4–6 minutes, or until the whites are set but the yolks are runny.
3. Sprinkle with the parsley and serve immediately from the pan with pitta or crusty bread.

MARY'S TIPS

The tomato base can be made up to 8 hours ahead. Heat before adding the eggs.

Not suitable for freezing.

Lentil Shepherd's Pie

This is a vegetarian version of a classic shepherd's pie. The lentils make a delicious, slightly nutty substitute for the usual minced lamb.

Serves 6–8

2 tbsp olive oil
2 onions, chopped
3 garlic cloves, finely grated
2 x 400g tins chopped tomatoes
600ml (1 pint) vegetable stock
250g (9oz) dried Puy lentils, rinsed
2 tbsp tomato purée
1–2 tbsp Worcestershire sauce
250g (9oz) spinach, any large leaves torn into smaller pieces
300g (10½oz) large chestnut mushrooms, thickly sliced

For the topping

1.2kg (2lb 10oz) floury potatoes (such as King Edward), peeled and cubed
Knob of butter
3–4 tbsp milk
115g (4oz) mature Cheddar, grated

1. You will need a 2 litre (3½ pint) ovenproof dish.
2. Heat the oil in a large, deep frying pan, add the onions and garlic and fry over a high heat for 3–4 minutes. Add the chopped tomatoes with the stock, lentils, tomato purée and Worcestershire sauce and bring to the boil. Cover with a lid and simmer over a low heat for 1 hour, or until the lentils are tender. Only once the lentils are tender, season with salt and freshly ground black pepper.
3. Add the spinach and mushrooms and stir over the heat until the spinach has wilted and the mushrooms are cooked. Tip into the ovenproof dish and set aside to cool.
4. Meanwhile, preheat the oven to 200°C/Fan 180°C/Gas 6.
5. Cook the potatoes in a pan of boiling salted water for 15–20 minutes until tender. Drain and return to the pan, add the butter and milk and mash until smooth, seasoning with salt and pepper. Spoon the mashed potato on top of the lentil mixture and sprinkle with the grated cheese. Place the dish on a baking tray in case it bubbles over, then bake in the oven for 30–35 minutes, or until golden and bubbling.

MARY'S TIPS

This dish can be assembled up to 12 hours ahead and left to cool completely, then cooked in the preheated oven for 30–40 minutes.

Otherwise, cool the assembled pie, then cover and freeze. Defrost fully and cook in the oven for 30–35 minutes until piping hot and golden.

Frittata with Spinach, Feta and Tomatoes

A wonderful brunch dish to feed the hungry. Change the cheese for mature Cheddar if you prefer.

Serves 4–6

2 tbsp olive oil
1 small onion, thinly sliced
½ red pepper, deseeded and diced
1 large garlic clove, finely grated
115g (4oz) baby spinach
8 large eggs
150g (5oz) feta, cut into small pieces
115g (4oz) cherry tomatoes, halved or quartered

1. You will need a 26cm (10½in) non-stick ovenproof frying pan. Preheat the oven to 200°C/Fan 180°C/Gas 6.
2. Heat the oil in the pan over a medium heat. Add the onion and pepper and fry gently for about 10 minutes, until the vegetables are tender, stirring occasionally. Add the garlic and spinach and fry for 2–3 minutes, until wilted. Leave the vegetables in the pan.
3. Meanwhile, beat the eggs in a jug and season well with salt and freshly ground black pepper. Pour into the pan and swirl around to coat the vegetables. Fry for 3–4 minutes, until the egg starts to set around the edges of the pan.
4. Scatter over the feta and tomatoes. Transfer to the preheated oven for about 10–15 minutes, until the egg is completely set in the middle and the frittata is lightly golden on top and underneath.
5. Slide on to a plate and slice into wedges to serve hot.

MARY'S TIPS

Best made and served.

Not suitable for freezing.

Salads and Sides

Avocado Caesar Salad

Roasted Red Pepper and Artichoke Salad

Superfood Salad

Burrata with Heritage Tomato Salad and Bloody Mary Dressing

Fiery Red Rice and Carrot Salad

Hot-smoked Salmon Rice and Asparagus Salad

Roasted Fennel, Onion and Potato with Parmesan Topping

Garlic Summer Veg

Pak Choi and Shiitake Stir-fry

Roasted Mediterranean Vegetables

Potato and Shallot Dauphinoise

Majorcan-style One Pot Vegetables

Split-roasted Butternut Squash with Chilli Garlic Butter

Posh Jacket Potatoes

Avocado Caesar Salad

A traditional Caesar salad dressing includes a raw or coddled egg, but I use mayonnaise here instead to give a creamy consistency. You could add crispy bacon and cooked chicken, if liked. Shaking the bread and oil in a bag is a top tip for getting crispy croûtons – if oil is simply poured over the bread in the frying pan, it can become soggy.

Serves 4–6

2 Romaine lettuces
55g (2oz) Parmesan shavings
1 x 50g tin anchovy fillets in oil, drained and halved (optional)
1 large avocado, peeled and sliced

For the sourdough croûtons

4 thick slices day-old sourdough or white bread
3 tbsp sunflower oil

For the Caesar dressing

100ml (3½fl oz) mayonnaise
Juice of ½ lemon
2 tsp Worcestershire sauce
30g (1oz) Parmesan, finely grated
1 garlic clove, finely grated
1 tbsp olive oil

1. First make the croûtons. Stack the slices of day-old bread and cut off the crusts. Cut the bread into 1cm (½in) cubes. Place the bread in a bowl or plastic bag with the sunflower oil and some salt and freshly ground black pepper. Mix well to coat (if you are using a bag, seal then shake it well).

2. Place a large non-stick frying pan over a medium heat. When the pan is hot, add the bread cubes and cook, stirring occasionally, until golden all over. Remove, drain on kitchen paper to remove excess oil, and set aside to cool.

3. To make the dressing, spoon the mayonnaise into a bowl. Add the lemon juice, Worcestershire sauce, Parmesan, garlic and seasoning. Gradually add the oil, whisking all the time, until well mixed.

4. Cut the lettuce into pieces and tip into a salad bowl. Add the Parmesan shavings, croûtons, anchovy fillets, if using, and avocado.

5. Pour over the dressing and toss to combine.

MARY'S TIPS

Croûtons can be made up to a week ahead. Assemble the salad to serve.

Not suitable for freezing.

Roasted Red Pepper and Artichoke Salad

A vibrant fresh salad full of colour – serve on a platter or in a bowl for best presentation.

Serves 4

300g (10½oz) roasted red peppers in oil, drained and sliced
175g (6oz) chargrilled artichoke hearts in oil, drained and cut into pieces
2 tsp shredded basil leaves
2 tsp balsamic vinegar

1. Mix the peppers and artichokes together in a bowl and season with salt and freshly ground black pepper. Add a little oil from the jar, if needed.
2. Add the basil leaves and balsamic vinegar and mix well.

MARY'S TIPS

Once made, the salad can be stored, covered, in the fridge for 1–2 days.

Not suitable for freezing.

Superfood Salad

A meal in itself – this is full of so much fresh flavour, varied texture and overall goodness!

Serves 4–6

100g (3½oz) long-grain brown rice (see tip)

1 × 400g tin green lentils, drained and rinsed (see tip)

1 large carrot, grated

½ red chilli, deseeded and finely diced

1 bunch of spring onions, sliced

Bunch of parsley, leaves chopped

250g (9oz) cooked beetroot, diced

For the dressing

2 tbsp white wine vinegar

4 tbsp olive oil

1 tsp caster sugar

1. Cook the rice in boiling water for about 25 minutes, or according to the packet instructions. Drain and refresh in cold water, then drain again.
2. Place the cooked rice and tinned lentils in a large bowl with the carrot, chilli, spring onions and parsley. Season with salt and freshly ground black pepper and mix together well.
3. Combine the dressing ingredients in a jug, then pour over the salad and toss to mix. Spoon into a serving bowl and scatter over the beetroot to serve.

MARY TIPS

Using pouches of ready-cooked rice will make this even quicker to prepare. You can substitute with 100g (3½oz) dried lentils, if you prefer. Cook them according to the packet instructions.

Can be made up to 6 hours ahead and stored in the fridge. Bring up to room temperature and add the beetroot to serve.

Not suitable for freezing.

Burrata with Heritage Tomato Salad and Bloody Mary Dressing

I find this is one of the most popular sharing plates – just break the burrata open and let everyone help themselves. Burrata, which means 'buttery' in Italian, is a fresh cheese made from a mix of mozzarella and cream. It's shaped like a ball and the outside thin shell is buffalo or cow's milk mozzarella, while the inside contains a soft, doughy, stringy mixture of curd and fresh cream. It's best served at room temperature.

Serves 4–6

750g (1lb 10oz) heritage tomatoes, mixed sizes and colours

1 large burrata ball (about 200g/7oz)

Small bunch of basil, leaves torn into pieces

Coarse sea salt, to taste

1 celery stick, with leaves

For the dressing

75ml (3fl oz) tomato juice

4 tbsp extra-virgin olive oil

1 tsp Worcestershire sauce

2 tsp balsamic vinegar

Tabasco sauce, to taste

Celery salt, to taste

1. Roughly slice the tomatoes into different shapes and sizes.
2. Place the burrata in the centre of a serving dish. Arrange the various tomatoes around the cheese and sprinkle with basil leaves.
3. For the dressing, mix the tomato juice, oil, Worcestershire sauce and vinegar in a jug and season well with Tabasco, celery salt and freshly ground black pepper.
4. To serve, season the tomatoes with coarse sea salt and pepper, and pour over a little of the dressing. Serve the rest of the dressing in a jug or bowl alongside. Add the celery stick and use it to stir the dressing, just before serving with some crusty bread.

MARY'S TIPS

Assemble the salad up to 2 hours ahead and dress just before serving.

The dressing can be made up to a day ahead.

Not suitable for freezing.

Fiery Red Rice and Carrot Salad

This is a great accompaniment to chargrilled meats, chicken or fish, so it's perfect for a summer BBQ. Camargue rice from France is a short-grained rice with a brownish-red colour, nutty flavour and slightly chewy texture, which can be found in most supermarkets. It takes about 30 minutes to simmer but should retain a little 'bite' when cooked.

Serves 10

450g (1lb) Camargue red rice

1 tsp salt

6 carrots, coarsely grated

8 spring onions, thinly sliced

Small bunch of coriander, leaves roughly chopped

For the dressing

Finely grated zest and juice of 4 limes

4 tsp clear runny honey

1–2 red chillies, finely chopped (see tip)

4 tbsp light olive oil

2 tbsp cider vinegar

1. Measure the rice into a jug, then tip into a saucepan with double the volume of boiling water – about 600ml (1 pint). Add the salt and bring back to the boil. Cover with a lid, reduce the heat and simmer gently for 20–30 minutes, until the grains are tender. Drain, if necessary, and set aside to cool.
2. Meanwhile, tip the carrots, spring onions and half the coriander into a mixing bowl.
3. Combine all the dressing ingredients in a jug and mix well.
4. Add the rice to the bowl of vegetables, then toss with the dressing. Taste and check the seasoning. Serve scattered with the remaining coriander.

MARY'S TIPS

Add as much or as little red chilli as you like. One red chilli is usually enough, but you can add a second if you like a bit of heat. If you have half a chilli left over, don't waste it – it can be frozen in a little plastic bag, then chopped and used from frozen.

The dish can be made up to 2 days ahead and kept in the fridge.

Not suitable for freezing.

Hot-smoked Salmon Rice and Asparagus Salad

Hot-smoked salmon is like poached salmon but with a smoky flavour – perfect for salads. Alternatively, you could use poached salmon. The lemon dressing and herbs make the salad vibrant and bursting with flavour.

Serves 6

300g (10½oz) mixed white and wild rice (see tip)

6 spring onions, finely sliced

Large bunch of dill, chopped

Large bunch of parsley, leaves chopped

3 eggs

200g (7oz) asparagus spears

200g (7oz) hot-smoked salmon slices, broken into large chunks

For the lemon dressing

Finely grated zest and juice of 1 lemon

100ml (3½fl oz) olive oil

2 tbsp white wine vinegar

2 tbsp runny honey

1 tbsp Dijon mustard

1. Cook the rice in boiling salted water according to the packet instructions. Drain and refresh under cold water. Drain again.
2. Place the rice in a bowl. Add the spring onions, dill and parsley and season well with salt and freshly ground black pepper. Stir to combine.
3. Measure all the dressing ingredients into a jug and whisk together well. Reserve 2 tablespoons of the dressing and pour the remainder over the rice. Mix well, cover with clingfilm and chill in the fridge for about an hour.
4. Meanwhile, place the eggs in a pan of boiling water and cook for 6–8 minutes for hard boiled with a soft middle. Drain and place in cold water before peeling. Cut each egg into quarters.
5. Remove the woody ends from the asparagus. If the spears are thick, cut them in half lengthways. Slice the spears into 5cm (2in) lengths, then cook in boiling water for 3 minutes. Drain and refresh under cold water. Drain again.
6. Tip the asparagus into the rice and mix to combine. Spoon into a serving dish and arrange the salmon pieces and egg quarters on top. Sprinkle with a little salt and freshly ground black pepper, then drizzle over the reserved dressing to serve.

MARY'S TIPS

Wild rice can be bought separately but it takes longer to cook than white. The wild rice in the mixed packets has been parboiled so both types cook for the same length of time. The salad can be assembled up to 4 hours ahead.

Not suitable for freezing.

Roasted Fennel, Onion and Potato with Parmesan Topping

This simple dish – a hearty combination of potatoes and vegetables – is all cooked in one dish so it's perfect for a dinner or Sunday lunch. In fact, it is so tasty you could eat it as a supper on its own, served with a lightly dressed salad.

Serves 6

3 large fennel bulbs
600g (1lb 5oz) large potatoes, peeled
3 onions, each cut into 6 wedges
55g (2oz) butter, plus extra for greasing
2 garlic cloves, finely grated
55g (2oz) Parmesan, grated

1. Preheat the oven to 200°C/Fan 180°C/Gas 6. Butter a shallow 2.5 litre (4 pint) ovenproof dish, about 23 x 30cm (9 x 12in).
2. Trim the tops from the fennel and cut each bulb in half through the root, then cut each in half lengthways into 3 wedges. Cut the potatoes into wedges the same size as the fennel wedges.
3. Bring a large pan of salted water to the boil, then cook the fennel and onions for about 5 minutes. Add the potatoes and boil for a further 5 minutes, until all the vegetables are just tender. Drain well.
4. Put the butter and the garlic in the empty vegetable pan and set over a low heat until just melted. Add the vegetables to the butter, toss until coated, then tip into the prepared dish. Sprinkle with the Parmesan and bake for 30–40 minutes, until piping hot.

MARY'S TIPS

It is essential to pre-cook the potatoes and fennel, otherwise they absorb too much butter and you'd have to use more, giving an over-rich result; the fennel would also be much tougher.

You can assemble the dish up to 12 hours ahead and chill in the fridge.

Not suitable for freezing.

Garlic Summer Veg

Quick and extremely simple. A wonderful all-in-one vegetable dish that is good to serve alongside chops or steaks.

Serves 4–6

- 2 tbsp sunflower oil
- 1 large onion, thinly sliced
- 1 red pepper, deseeded and sliced
- 30g (1oz) butter
- 1 garlic clove, finely grated
- 400g (14oz) small courgettes, thinly sliced
- Juice of ½ lemon

1. Heat the oil in a large frying pan or wok over a high heat. Add the onion and pepper and fry for about 4–5 minutes, until soft and lightly golden.
2. Add the butter and garlic and fry for 30 seconds. Add the courgettes and fry for 2 minutes, until just cooked but firm.
3. Season well with salt and freshly ground black pepper, pour over the lemon juice and serve at once.

MARY'S TIPS

Best made and served.

Not suitable for freezing.

Pak Choi and Shiitake Stir-fry

Also known as bok choy, pak choi is a Chinese cabbage with broad, white, succulent stems and mildly mustard-flavoured green leaves. It looks something like Swiss chard and I cook it in a similar way, slicing off the leaves and cooking the stem end separately. In this recipe there is the option to cook the stems and add the sliced leaves 2 or 3 minutes before the end of cooking; or keep the leaves, cook them like spinach and serve with a later meal.

Serves 4

2 tbsp sesame or sunflower oil

1 small red pepper, deseeded and sliced

12 thin spring onions, trimmed

2 sticks of lemongrass, bulb section only, finely chopped

1 small red chilli, deseeded and thinly sliced

2 fat garlic cloves, finely grated

2.5cm (1in) piece of fresh root ginger, peeled and cut into slivers

450g (1lb) pak choi, sliced, keeping the white and green parts separate

175g (6oz) shiitake mushrooms, sliced

2 tbsp oyster sauce

Dash of dark soy sauce

1. Heat the oil in a large wok or frying pan. When hot, add the pepper, spring onions, lemongrass, chilli, garlic and ginger, and toss constantly over a high heat for about 1 minute.
2. Add the white pak choi and mushrooms, and continue to fry, briskly tossing the vegetables for a further minute. Stir in the oyster sauce and pak choi leaves. Add a dash of soy sauce to season.
3. Toss and cook only for as long as it takes to get everything piping hot. Check the seasoning and serve immediately.

MARY'S TIPS

Be careful with the chilli. Handle it as little as possible and wash your hands thoroughly after preparing it, or wear rubber gloves if you prefer.

Have all the raw ingredients prepared and ready to cook: you can keep them chilled for up to 6 hours before cooking.

Not suitable for freezing.

Roasted Mediterranean Vegetables

These roasted veg are a great side dish or you could double up quantities to serve them as a main meal.

Serves 6

- 4 tbsp olive oil
- 1 small aubergine, sliced into thick half-moons
- 1 large red pepper, deseeded and cut into chunks
- 1 red onion, sliced into wedges
- 250g (9oz) butternut squash, cut into 2cm (¾in) cubes (prepared weight)
- 3 garlic cloves, skin on
- 3 sprigs of thyme
- 200g (7oz) baby courgettes or 1 large courgette, thickly sliced
- 1 tbsp balsamic glaze

1. Preheat the oven to 220°C/Fan 200°C/Gas 7.
2. Measure 3 tablespoons of the oil into a large roasting tin and preheat in the oven for a few minutes to get hot.
3. Remove the tin from the oven and add the aubergines, pepper, onion and squash, and toss carefully in the hot oil. Scatter over the garlic cloves and thyme sprigs and season well with salt and freshly ground black pepper. Roast in the oven for 15–20 minutes.
4. Add the courgettes and roast for another 12–15 minutes, or until all the vegetables are tender and golden.
5. Snip off the end of the garlic cloves and squeeze out the soft garlic from their skins. Mix into the veg. Discard the thyme sprigs, check the seasoning and toss everything together. Drizzle with the remaining oil and the balsamic glaze to serve.

MARY'S TIPS

The veg can be made up to the end of roasting up to 6 hours ahead.

Not suitable for freezing.

Potato and Shallot Dauphinoise

Completely delicious and indulgent. Perfect to make ahead, then pop in the oven.

Serves 6

Butter, for greasing
2 tbsp sunflower oil
4 banana shallots, sliced
2 garlic cloves, finely grated
1kg (2lb 4oz) floury potatoes, such as King Edward, peeled and thinly sliced
300ml (½ pint) double cream
450ml (¾ pint) chicken or vegetable stock
100g (3½oz) Gruyère or mature Cheddar, grated

1. Preheat the oven to 200°C/Fan 180°C/Gas 6 and generously butter a 2 litre (3½ pint) shallow ovenproof dish.
2. Place the oil in a frying pan over a low heat. Add the shallots, cover with a lid and fry for 8-10 minutes, until soft. Add the garlic and fry for 30 seconds. Set aside.
3. Arrange one layer of sliced potatoes in the buttered dish. Season with salt and freshly ground black pepper, then scatter over some of the shallots and garlic. Drizzle over a little double cream and stock. Continue to layer the potatoes, onion, garlic and cream and stock until you have used them all.
4. Push the potatoes down into the liquid using your hands so they are all covered, then cover with foil and bake in the preheated the oven for about 45 minutes. Remove the foil and sprinkle with the cheese. Continue to cook for another 25–30 minutes, or until golden brown and the potatoes are cooked through.
5. Leave to stand for 5 minutes before serving.

MARY'S TIPS

Can be assembled up to 8 hours ahead. Best cooked to serve.

Not for freezing.

Majorcan-style One Pot Vegetables

A rustic dish of layered of potatoes, aubergines and peppers. Double up the recipe if there's a crowd. This is good to cook ahead as it reheats well.

Serves 6

2 large aubergines, sliced into rounds about 2cm (¾in) thick

Olive oil, for cooking and drizzling

3 red peppers, deseeded and cut into pieces

700g (1lb 9oz) potatoes, peeled and cut into cubes

2 tsp ground cumin

2 onions, finely chopped

½–1 red chilli, deseeded and finely chopped

2 large garlic cloves, finely grated

2 × 400g tin chopped tomatoes

1 tbsp tomato purée

Dash of sugar

Small bunch of coriander, leaves chopped (optional)

MARY'S TIPS

Can be made a day ahead and reheated.

Not suitable for freezing.

1. Preheat the oven to 220°C/Fan 200°C/Gas 7 and line two large baking sheets with non-stick baking paper.
2. Place the slices of aubergine on one of the baking sheets in a single layer. Brush both sides with olive oil and season with salt and freshly ground black pepper. Place the peppers in one half of the second baking sheet and the potatoes on the other side. Drizzle both with oil and season. Place both baking sheets in the oven and roast for 30 minutes, until the vegetables are soft and tinged brown. Sprinkle the ground cumin over the potatoes and toss lightly together.
3. Reduce the oven temperature to 200°C/Fan 180°C/Gas 6.
4. Heat 2 tablespoons of olive oil in a large saucepan over a high heat. Add the onions and fry for about 3–4 minutes. Add the chilli and garlic and fry for a few seconds. Stir in the chopped tomatoes, purée and sugar and bring to the boil. Cover with a lid, reduce the heat and simmer for about 10 minutes. Season well.
5. Place half the potatoes in the base of an ovenproof dish. Scatter over the peppers and arrange a neat row of aubergines on top. Spoon half the tomato sauce over the vegetables and sprinkle with half the coriander, if using. Repeat with a second layer of potatoes, peppers and aubergines, finishing with a layer of tomato sauce. Cover with foil and bake in the preheated oven for 30 minutes.
6. Remove the foil and sprinkle with the remaining coriander, if using, to serve.

Split-roasted Butternut Squash with Chilli Garlic Butter

I love all squash, but I particularly enjoy the nutty flavour of the butternut and its lovely vibrant colour.

Serves 4–6

1 butternut squash
1–2 tbsp olive oil, for drizzling
55g (2oz) butter, softened
1 tbsp freshly chopped parsley
1 tbsp chopped chives
1 small garlic clove, finely grated
½ red chilli, deseeded and finely diced

1. Preheat the oven to 220°C/Fan 200°C/Gas 7.

2. Slice the squash in half lengthways and scoop out the seeds. Sit the halves, cut-side up, in a roasting tin. Season well with salt and freshly ground black pepper and drizzle with olive oil.

3. Pour 300ml (½ pint) water into the base of the tin around the squash. Roast in the preheated oven for about 45–60 minutes, depending on the size of the squash, or until the flesh is soft.

4. While the squash is roasting, mash the butter with the herbs, garlic and chilli. Place the butter on a piece of clingfilm and roll the clingfilm around the butter to make a cylinder. Seal the ends and chill in the fridge for 30 minutes.

5. When the squash is cooked and golden, slice the butter into rounds and place on top of the squash to melt gently. Serve the squash on wooden boards with spoons for scooping out.

MARY'S TIPS

Chilli garlic butter can be made up to a week ahead.

Chilli garlic butter freezes well.

Posh Jacket Potatoes

These have a lovely filling to make a change from plain jacket potatoes.

Serves 4

4 large baking potatoes, scrubbed clean

About 4 tbsp pouring double cream

Knob of butter

100g (3½oz) mature Cheddar, coarsely grated

115g (4oz) sun-blushed tomatoes, finely chopped

4 spring onions, finely sliced

A little olive oil, for drizzling (optional)

1. Preheat the oven to 220°C/Fan 200°C/Gas 7.
2. Prick the potatoes, then place in the oven and bake for about 1 hour, or until soft in the middle.
3. Slice each potato in half and scoop out the soft centre into a bowl. Add the remaining ingredients to the bowl, season with salt and freshly ground black pepper, and mix to combine.
4. Spoon the mixture back into the skins, then arrange the potatoes cut-side up in a roasting tin. Drizzle with some sun-blushed tomato oil, or a little olive oil, and return to the oven to 15–20 minutes, or until golden and the skins are crips.
5. Serve straight from the oven.

MARY'S TIPS

The potatoes can be filled and ready for their second bake up to 4 hours ahead. To reheat, roast at the same temperature for 30 minutes – you may need to cover with foil if the top is getting too brown.

Not suitable for freezing.

Baking

Coffee Latte Traybake

Stem Ginger Shortbread

Hummingbird Cake

Bara Brith

Blueberry Muffins

Orange Polenta Cake

Lemon and Passion Fruit Traybake

Very Best Chocolate Fudge Cake

Red Velvet Cupcakes

Flapjacks

Banana Loaf

Harvest Fruit Cake

Salted Caramel Brownies

Focaccia with Olives, Tomatoes and Rosemary

Cheese and Garlic Tear-and-share Scones

Nordic Seed and Nut Loaf

Coffee Latte Traybake

A creamy coffee traybake, just like a latte coffee. Traybakes are the most useful of cakes, whether they are for lunch boxes, children's parties or for friends, as they are easy to cook and easy to store.

Makes 12–16 pieces

For the coffee cake

2 tbsp instant coffee granules
2 tbsp boiling water
225g (8oz) baking spread, straight from the fridge, plus extra for greasing
225g (8oz) light muscovado sugar
225g (8oz) self-raising flour
1 tsp baking powder
4 large eggs

For the mascarpone icing

1 tsp instant coffee granules
1–2 tsp boiling water
75g (3oz) butter, softened
100g (3½oz) full-fat mascarpone
200g (7oz) icing sugar

1. Preheat the oven to 180°C/Fan 160°C/Gas 4. Grease the base and sides of a 23 × 30cm (9 × 12in) traybake tin and line with non-stick baking paper.
2. To make the cake, measure the coffee granules into a large bowl and add the boiling water. Stir to dissolve. Measure all the remaining cake ingredients into the bowl and whisk using an electric whisk until light and fluffy.
3. Spoon the sponge mixture into the tin and level the surface. Bake in the preheated oven for 30–35 minutes, or until well risen and springing back when pressed in the centre.
4. Leave to cool in the tin for 10 minutes, then carefully turn out, discard the lining paper and set aside to cool completely on a wire rack.
5. To make the icing, dissolve the coffee in the boiling water in a small bowl and mix until smooth. Measure the butter into a large bowl or free-standing mixer and whisk with an electric whisk to soften. Add the mascarpone, dissolved coffee and icing sugar, and whisk again until smooth and creamy.
6. Spread over the traybake and swirl the top. Slice into pieces to serve.

MARY'S TIPS

Baking spread gives an excellent result but must be used straight from the fridge. If you wish to use butter, make sure it is soft before mixing.

Can be made up to a day ahead and iced on the day. Freezes well un-iced.

Stem Ginger Shortbread

For me, shortbread is the ultimate biscuit – a favourite in every way. I serve these each week after a game of tennis with my girlfriends – we chat more than we play, I have to admit, but it is fun and helps keep me fit!

Makes 30

- 5 balls of stem ginger in syrup, drained and finely chopped
- 225g (8oz) plain flour, plus extra for dusting
- 225g (8oz) butter, cut into cubes
- 115g (4oz) caster sugar
- 115g (4oz) semolina
- 2 tbsp demerara sugar

1. You will need a 23 x 33cm (9 x 13in) traybake tin. Preheat the oven to 160°C/Fan 140°C/Gas 3.
2. Dry the chopped ginger thoroughly with kitchen paper to absorb all the excess syrup.
3. Measure the flour, butter, caster sugar and semolina into a large bowl and rub together with your fingertips, or whiz in a food processor for a few minutes, until the mixture comes together in a very crumbly dough. Tip on to a lightly floured worktop and knead in the chopped ginger.
4. Press the dough into the traybake tin and, using the back of a spoon, level the surface. Sprinkle with the demerara sugar, then bake in the oven for 40 minutes, or until very pale golden and firm to the touch.
5. Leave to cool for 5 minutes in the tin, then cut the shortbread into 30 even-sized fingers or triangles (see tip). Carefully remove from the tin (see tip) and transfer to a wire rack to cool completely.

MARY'S TIPS

To make shortbread triangles, cut 5 × 3 lines across the tin and slice each square in half diagonally to give 30 triangles.

You must remove the biscuits from the tin as soon as they have been cut and just cooled, or they will stick.

Can be made up to 3 days ahead and kept in an airtight container in between layers of kitchen paper to prevent them from sticking. The cooked shortbread freezes well. Refresh in a moderate oven for about 10 minutes (no need to defrost first).

Hummingbird Cake

The addition of pineapple in this Southern US classic takes banana cake up a notch. It makes for a moist, substantial cake, beautifully offset by the tangy cream cheese icing.

Serves 8–10

For the sponge
- 250g (9oz) self-raising flour
- 250g (9oz) caster sugar
- 1 tsp baking powder
- 1 tsp ground cinnamon
- 55g (2oz) walnut pieces, chopped
- 2 large ripe bananas, peeled and mashed (200–250g/7–9oz peeled weight)
- 1 × 432g tin pineapple chunks, drained and finely chopped
- 2 eggs, beaten
- 1 tsp vanilla extract
- 175ml (6fl oz) sunflower oil, plus extra for greasing

For the icing
- 115g (4oz) butter, softened
- 175g (6oz) full-fat cream cheese (see tip)
- 300g (10½oz) icing sugar, sifted
- 1 tsp vanilla extract

1. You will need two 20cm (8in) round, loose-bottomed sandwich tins. Preheat the oven to 200°C/Fan 180°C/Gas 6 and grease the tins with a little sunflower oil, then line the bases of each with a disc of non-stick baking paper.

2. Measure the flour, sugar, baking powder and cinnamon into a large bowl, add the chopped walnut pieces and stir together. In a separate bowl, mix together the bananas, pineapple, eggs, vanilla extract and sunflower oil. Add the banana/pineapple mixture to the dry ingredients and stir with a wooden spoon to combine, taking care not to overmix.

3. Divide the batter evenly between the prepared tins, smoothing the surfaces with a spoon. Bake in the preheated oven for about 25–30 minutes or until golden, well risen and springy to the touch. Set aside to cool down completely before turning out and peeling off the paper.

4. To make the icing, place the butter in a bowl with the cream cheese, icing sugar and vanilla extract and beat together with an electric hand whisk until smooth. It is best to beat in the icing sugar a little at a time, so that it doesn't fly everywhere. Chill the icing for 30 minutes before assembling the cake.

5. To assemble the cake, place one cold sponge on a plate or cake stand, and spread with half the icing. Sit the other sponge on top and spread with the remaining icing.

MARY'S TIPS

Take the cream cheese out of the fridge to soften before making the icing, or beat to soften first.

The cake will keep for 1–2 days at a cool room temperature. The sponges freeze well.

Bara Brith

This is a classic Welsh teabread, so easy to make as it is all in one and it also keeps well. Literally translated it means 'speckled bread', presumably due to its appearance.

Makes 1 loaf

300ml (½ pint) strong tea of your choice
90g (3½oz) sultanas
90g (3½oz) raisins
90g (3½oz) dried cranberries
90g (3½oz) currants
Butter, for greasing
½ tsp ground mixed spice
225g (8oz) light muscovado sugar
275g (10oz) self-raising flour
1 egg, beaten

1. Make the tea in a teapot, then pour it into a large heatproof bowl. Add all the fruits and stir to coat. Cover and leave for minimum of 6 hours or overnight to allow the fruit to absorb the tea and plump up.
2. Preheat the oven to 160°C/Fan 140°C/Gas 3. Grease and line a 900g (2lb) loaf tin with non-stick baking paper.
3. Add the spice, sugar, flour and egg to the fruits and mix well. Spoon into the prepared tin and level the surface. Bake in the preheated oven for about 1½ hours, until well risen and firm to the touch. Insert a skewer into middle of the cake; if it comes out clean then the loaf is ready. Leave in the tin to cool for 10 minutes before turning out onto a wire rack to cool completely.
4. Slice into fairly thick slices and spread with butter to serve. Add some red jam as well, if liked!

MARY'S TIPS

Can be made up to 3 days ahead.

Freezes well.

Blueberry Muffins

These are like the traditional American muffins so don't expect them to be very sweet. They are always best served warm.

Makes 12

275g (10oz) self-raising flour
1 tsp baking powder
2 eggs
75g (3oz) caster sugar
225ml (8fl oz) milk
115g (4oz) butter, melted and cooled slightly
1 tsp vanilla extract
175g (6oz) fresh blueberries

1. Preheat the oven to 200°C/Fan 180°C/Gas 6 and line a 12-hole muffin tin with paper cases.
2. Measure all the ingredients except the blueberries into a bowl and mix with a wooden spoon until just combined. Take care not to overwork the mixture. Stir in the blueberries, then divide evenly between the paper cases.
3. Bake in the middle of the preheated oven for 20–25 minutes, or until risen, cooked through and lightly golden.
4. Remove to a wire rack to cool slightly before serving.

MARY'S TIPS

Best made to serve.

Freeze well.

Orange Polenta Cake

This cake batter is quite stiff compared to a normal sponge cake batter. Gluten-free, expect it to be firm and grainy due to its flourless nature and the ground almonds.

Serves 8–10

300g (10½oz) butter, softened, plus extra for greasing
300g (10½oz) caster sugar
Finely grated zest and juice of 1 orange
4 eggs, beaten
300g (10½oz) ground almonds
150g (5oz) fine polenta (see tip)
1 tsp baking powder

For the glaze
Finely grated zest and juice of 1 large orange
75g (3oz) caster sugar

1. Preheat the oven to 160°C/Fan 140°C/Gas 3, then grease a 23cm (9in) round springform cake tin with butter and line the base with a disc of non-stick baking paper.
2. Measure the butter and sugar into a bowl, add the orange zest and beat with an electric hand whisk until pale and fluffy. Whisk in the eggs a little bit at a time (this may look curdled, but do not worry), then add the ground almonds, polenta, orange juice and baking powder, and carefully fold until thoroughly combined. It will be a thick mixture. Spoon into the prepared tin and level the surface.
3. Bake in the preheated oven for about 1¼ hours, or until golden brown and springy to the touch and a skewer inserted into the middle of the cake comes out clean. Allow to cool down a little in the tin while you make the glaze.
4. Place the orange zest and juice in a small saucepan with the sugar. Stir together over a low heat, then raise the heat and stir until the sugar has dissolved. Spoon the hot syrup over the warm cake and leave to cool completely in the tin (see tip).
5. Serve in wedges with a dollop of crème fraîche.

MARY'S TIPS

Choose a finely ground polenta, if possible, rather than a coarser grain, which would be a bit too rough for this cake.

Spoon over the warm syrup evenly so that the orange zest decorates the cake.

Can be made up to a day ahead. Freezes well.

Lemon and Passion Fruit Traybake

Traybakes are so versatile and are perfect for sharing or wrapping as gifts. Passion fruit curd is readily available and it is wonderful to be able to buy it so easily, as we love it! This recipe also works well with lemon or orange curd instead of passion fruit.

Makes 16 pieces

225g (8oz) baking spread, straight from the fridge, plus extra for greasing
225g (8oz) caster sugar
275g (10oz) self-raising flour
1 tsp baking powder
4 eggs
2 tbsp milk
2 tbsp passion fruit curd
Finely grated zest of 2 lemons

For the passion icing

300ml (½ pint) pouring double cream
4 tbsp passion fruit curd

1. Preheat the oven to 180°C/Fan 160°C/Gas 4. Grease and line a 30 × 23cm (12 × 9in) traybake tin with non-stick baking paper.

2. Measure all the traybake ingredients into a large bowl and beat with an electric hand whisk until combined and smooth.

3. Spoon the cake mixture into the prepared tin and level the top. Bake in the preheated oven for about 35 minutes, or until the cake has shrunk from the sides of the tin and springs back when pressed in the centre. Leave to cool in the tin.

4. To make the passion icing, combine the cream and half the curd in a large bowl and whip until soft peaks. (Be careful not to overwhip, as the curd will make it thick.) Spread the icing over the surface of the cooled cake.

5. Drizzle the top of the traybake with the remaining curd (see tip) in a zig-zag pattern. Cut into 16 pieces to serve.

MARY'S TIPS

If your curd is very thick, you could loosen it with a little water, or warm it gently, in order to drizzle it to decorate it at the end.

Can be made up to a day ahead. Freezes well un-iced.

If you overwhip the cream and it starts to curdle, save it by adding a little more liquid cream, a spoonful at a time, until it becomes smooth again.

Very Best Chocolate Fudge Cake

This will become your favourite chocolate cake recipe! It is speedy to make and the easy filling doubles as an icing. The cake is moist and has a 'grown-up' chocolate flavour. No need to sieve the apricot jam, it's nice to come across the odd lump of apricot.

Serves 8–10

75g (3oz) cocoa powder, sifted
8 tbsp boiling water
3 large eggs
50ml (2fl oz) milk
175g (6oz) self-raising flour
1 tsp baking powder
115g (4oz) baking spread straight from the fridge
275g (10oz) caster sugar

For the icing and filling

150g (5oz) Bournville chocolate, chopped into small pieces
150ml (¼ pint) pouring double cream
3 generous tbsp apricot jam

1. Preheat the oven to 180°C/Fan 160°C/Gas 4. Grease two 20cm (8in) deep sandwich tins then line the base of each tin with non-stick baking paper.
2. Blend the cocoa and boiling water in a large bowl, until a smooth paste. Add the remaining cake ingredients and beat until a smooth, loose batter.
3. Divide the mixture equally between the prepared tins and level the surface. Bake in the oven for about 30 minutes, or until well risen and the tops spring back when pressed with a finger. Leave to cool in the tins for a few minutes, then turn out, peel off the paper and finish cooling on a wire rack.
4. Warm the apricot jam in a very small pan, then spread a little over the base of one cake and the top of the other.
5. To make the icing, tip the chocolate into a large bowl. Place the cream in a pan over a medium heat and warm until just below boiling point. Pour the cream over the chocolate and leave for a couple of minutes before whisking to combine. Leave to cool completely, until thick and a spreadable consistency. Use a small palette knife to spread half the icing over one of the cakes. Sandwich the other cake on top, then spread the remaining icing over the top. Keep in a cool place until ready to serve.

MARY'S TIPS

Store in a container about 2.5cm (1in) bigger than the diameter of the cake. Sit the cake on the inside of the lid and place the container over the top. The cake can be frozen (iced or un-iced). If the cake is frozen iced, the icing will not be as shiny once defrosted. To defrost, thaw for 4 hours.

Red Velvet Cupcakes

These taste as good as they look – moist chocolate sponge with a tangy cream cheese icing. The velvety red colour is obtained from a food-colouring gel, which yields stronger results than a liquid food colouring.

Makes 12

For the cupcakes

115g (4oz) butter, softened

150g (5oz) caster sugar

125g (4½oz) self-raising flour

25g (1oz) cocoa powder, sifted, plus extra for dusting

2 eggs

2 tbsp milk

2 tsp red natural food-colouring gel

For the frosting

55g (2oz) butter, softened

200g (7oz) full-fat cream cheese

300g (10½oz) icing sugar, sifted

½ tsp vanilla extract

1. You will need a 12-hole muffin tin and a piping bag fitted with a star nozzle (optional). Preheat the oven to 180°C/Fan 160°C/Gas 4 and line the tin with paper cases.

2. Measure all the cupcake ingredients into a large bowl and mix together until smooth, either by hand or using an electric hand whisk or food mixer (see tip). Spoon the batter into the paper cases, dividing it evenly between them.

3. Bake in the oven for 20–25 minutes until well risen and springy to the touch. Remove the cupcakes from the tin and leave to cool on a wire rack.

4. To make the frosting, measure all the ingredients into a food processor and whiz until smooth, or beat together with an electric hand whisk. Fill the piping bag (if using) with the frosting (see tip) and pipe the frosting on to the cooled cupcakes. Alternatively, add the frosting to the cakes using a teaspoon, spreading it over the tops. Dust the cupcakes with cocoa powder to serve.

MARY'S TIPS

If using an electric hand whisk or food mixer to make the sponge, do not overmix or this may result in flat cakes.

Stand the icing bag in a tall jug with the top of the bag folded over the side to make it easier to fill with the frosting. Make sure the end of the bag is twisted closed as you pipe the frosting on to the cakes so it doesn't leak out.

Can be made up to a day ahead and frosted to serve. Cupcakes freeze well without the frosting.

Flapjacks

Adored by all ages and perfect for the biscuit tin. I like them with a little softness in the centre, not too brittle.

Makes 24

150g (5oz) butter, cubed, plus extra for greasing
150g (5oz) light muscovado sugar
150g (5oz) golden syrup
1 tsp vanilla extract
225g (8oz) rolled oats

1. Preheat the oven to 180°C/Fan 160°C/Gas 4, then grease a 18cm (7in) square, solid-based, deep-sided baking tin with butter and line the base with non-stick baking paper.
2. Measure the butter, sugar and syrup into a saucepan (see tip). Slowly melt over a low heat, stirring until the butter is melted and the sugar has dissolved. Remove from the heat, then add the vanilla and oats, and stir to combine.
3. Spoon into the prepared tin and level the top. Bake in the preheated oven for about 30 minutes, or until firm to the touch around the edges but still a little soft in the centre. Remove from the oven and leave to cool in the tin for about 10 minutes. Score the flapjack into 24 pieces, using a small sharp knife, then leave to finish cooling in the tin.
4. Once completely cool, turn out, remove the paper and cut along the score lines to make 24 pieces.

MARY'S TIPS

Golden syrup is readily available in squeezy bottles, which makes it easy to measure out. If it's in the traditional tin, use a greased spoon for measuring so that it slips off easily.

Flapjacks freeze well.

Banana Loaf

This is a lovely moist loaf, which really doesn't need to be buttered. Any bananas left in the fruit bowl are ideal for this cake – the riper they are, the better.

Makes 1 loaf

115g (4oz) baking spread, straight from the fridge
175g (6oz) caster sugar
2 large eggs
3 ripe bananas, mashed (225g/8oz prepared weight)
225g (8oz) self-raising flour
1 tsp baking powder
2 tbsp milk

1. Preheat the oven to 180°C/Fan 160°C/Gas 4. Lightly grease and line the base and sides of a 900g (2lb) loaf tin with non-stick baking paper.

2. Measure all the ingredients into a mixing bowl and beat with an electric hand whisk until well blended.

3. Spoon the mixture into the prepared tin and level the surface. Bake in the preheated oven for about 1–1¼ hours, until well risen and golden brown. Keep checking on the loaf, to make sure it isn't getting too dark. Cover it with foil once it is golden brown. It is ready when a fine skewer inserted in the centre comes out clean.

4. Leave to cool in the tin for a few minutes, then turn out, peel off the baking paper and finish cooling on a wire rack.

5. Slice thickly to serve.

MARY'S TIPS

Best made to serve.

Freezes well.

Harvest Fruit Cake

A delicious fruit cake that takes no time at all to prepare. Be sure to use the right size tin as it is a deep cake; a different-sized tin would affect the cooking time.

Serves 8–10

115g (4oz) red or natural glacé cherries, quartered
225g (8oz) butter, softened
225g (8oz) light muscovado sugar
4 large eggs
250g (9oz) self-raising flour
2 tsp ground mixed spice
225g (8oz) sultanas
115g (4oz) currants
55g (2oz) candied mixed peel, chopped
Finely grated zest of 2 lemons

1. Preheat the oven to 160°C/Fan 140°C/Gas 3. Grease and line the base and sides of a 20cm (8in) deep round cake tin with non-stick baking paper.
2. Place the cherries in a sieve and rinse under running water. Drain them well, then dry thoroughly on kitchen paper.
3. Measure the butter, sugar, eggs, flour and mixed spice into a large mixing bowl and beat with an electric hand whisk until thoroughly blended. Add all the remaining ingredients and mix well.
4. Spoon the mixture into the prepared tin and level the surface. Bake in the preheated oven for about 2¼–2½ hours, until well risen, evenly brown and firm to the touch. Cover with foil after 1½ hours if the top is browning too quickly.
5. Leave to cool in the tin for 10 minutes then turn out, peel off the baking paper and finish cooling on a wire rack.

MARY'S TIPS

Can be made up to 3 days ahead.

Freezes well.

Salted Caramel Brownies

I have never been too keen on salted caramel, but I am beginning to like it! I know it is loved by many, hence using it for a couple of recipes.

Makes 24 pieces

- 360g (12½oz) dark chocolate, broken into pieces
- 225g (8oz) butter, cubed, plus extra for greasing
- 225g (8oz) light muscovado sugar
- 4 eggs, beaten
- 75g (3oz) self-raising flour
- 1 tsp vanilla extract
- 200g (7oz) salted caramel sauce from a jar
- Pinch of Maldon sea salt
- 75g (3oz) Biscoff biscuits, each broken into 3 pieces

1. Preheat the oven to 180°C/Fan 160°C/Gas 4. Grease and line a 30 × 23cm (12 × 9in) traybake tin with non-stick baking paper.
2. Place the chocolate and butter in a large heatproof bowl. Place the bowl over a pan of simmering water until melted, being careful that the bottom of the bowl does not touch the water. Stir to combine.
3. Remove from the heat and add the sugar and eggs. Mix well until smooth, then add the flour and vanilla and mix again.
4. Place the caramel sauce and sea salt in a small bowl and mix well.
5. Pour the chocolate mixture into the prepared tin. Drizzle the salted caramel sauce over the top in a swirly pattern, then scatter with the biscuits, pressing them down slightly. Bake in the preheated oven for about 40–45 minutes, or until well risen and set around the edges, with a slightly soft centre.
6. Leave to cool in the tin, then slice into 24 pieces.

MARY'S TIP

Can be made up to 2 days ahead.

Freeze well.

Focaccia with Olives, Tomatoes and Rosemary

Bread is a natural comfort food. As a nation we eat slightly less of it now, so it is such a treat to make your own.

Makes 1 loaf

- 450g (1lb) strong white bread flour, plus extra for dusting
- 1 × 7g packet fast-action dried yeast
- 1 tbsp olive oil, plus extra for greasing
- ½ tsp salt
- 1 tsp caster sugar
- 300ml (½ pint) warm (not hot) water
- 1 egg, beaten

For the flavouring

- 150g (5oz) pitted olives, roughly chopped
- 100g (3½oz) sun-dried tomatoes, roughly chopped
- 100g (3½oz) Parmesan, finely grated
- 2 garlic cloves, finely grated
- 1 sprig of rosemary
- Flaky sea salt, to finish

1. Lightly grease a 23 × 33cm (9 × 13in) Swiss roll tin with oil.
2. To make the dough, measure the flour, yeast, oil, salt, sugar and water into a free-standing food mixer. Using the dough hook on medium speed, mix until you have a smooth dough (about 5 minutes). Alternatively, combine in a bowl and knead by hand for 10–15 minutes.
3. Grease a large bowl with oil. Add the dough, cover with clingfilm, and leave to rise in a warm place for about 1–1½ hours, or until doubled in size.
4. Tip the dough out onto a floured work surface. Knead for 3–4 minutes, then add the olives, tomatoes, cheese and garlic. Knead together until everything is incorporated.
5. Place the dough in the prepared tin and push out to fill the tin. Snip the rosemary into little sprigs and insert them into the dough, arranging them evenly over the top. Place the tin in a clean plastic bag and leave to prove in a warm place for about 30 minutes, until light and puffy. Preheat the oven to 220°C/Fan 200°C/Gas 7.
6. Brush with the beaten egg and sprinkle with some sea salt. Bake for 25–30 minutes until well risen and golden brown on top and underneath.
7. Slice and serve with olive oil and balsamic vinegar for dipping.

MARY'S TIPS

Can be made a day ahead but best made fresh.
Freezes well once cooked.

Cheese and Garlic Tear-and-share Scones

These deliciously cheesy scones would be lovely for lunch to accompany soup, and a 'tear-and-share' loaf is perfect for informal eating. Using a scone rather than a yeast dough means they are quicker to make too.

Serves 10–12

450g (1lb) self-raising flour, plus extra for dusting
2 tsp baking powder
2 tsp mustard powder
1 tsp salt
115g (4oz) butter, cubed
55g (2oz) Parmesan, finely grated, plus extra for sprinkling
115g (4oz) mature Cheddar, grated
1 garlic clove, finely grated
6 tbsp finely snipped chives
2 eggs
About 150ml (¼ pint) milk

1. Preheat the oven to 220°C/Fan 200°C/Gas 7 and line a baking sheet with non-stick baking paper.
2. Measure the flour and baking powder into a large bowl with the mustard, salt and butter. Using your fingertips, rub in the butter until the mixture resembles fine breadcrumbs. Add both cheeses with the garlic and chives.
3. Beat the eggs in a jug, adding enough milk to make up to 300ml (½ pint) of liquid. Gradually add this to the mixture in the bowl and mix together to make a dough (see tip). Tip on to a lightly floured work surface and knead until smooth, then divide into 22 equal-sized balls.
4. Arrange the balls of dough on the prepared baking sheet to form a round with all the balls just touching. Brush with any leftover milk and sprinkle with the extra Parmesan.
5. Bake in the oven for 25 minutes until well risen and golden on top and underneath. Serve warm with butter.

MARY'S TIP

A scone dough should be fairly sticky rather than dry. If it is on the wet side, it gives a better rise and the resulting scones are very moist.

Can be made up to a day ahead.

Freeze well.

Nordic Seed and Nut Loaf

This feels so healthy and is a delicious combination of close firm texture and nutty flavour. Chia seeds are an edible seed from a plant native to Mexico and related to the mint family; they are very high in fibre and have health benefits. Swap the dates for cranberries or figs, if liked – using the same amount. This is great spread with butter and served with gravadlax or smoked salmon, charcuterie, cheese and pickles, or as a base for canapés.

Makes 1 loaf

- Butter or oil, for greasing
- 4 large eggs
- 3 tbsp olive oil
- 55g (2oz) soft dried dates, finely chopped
- ¼ tsp sea salt
- 75g (3oz) pumpkin seeds
- 75g (3oz) sunflower seeds
- 150g (5oz) pecans, chopped
- 55g (2oz) sesame seeds
- 3 tbsp chia seeds

1. Preheat the oven to 180°C/Fan 160°C/Gas 4. Grease and line the base and sides of a 900g (2lb) loaf tin with non-stick baking paper.
2. Break the eggs into a bowl and beat with a fork until combined. Add all the remaining ingredients and mix well using a wooden spoon.
3. Pour the mixture into the prepared loaf tin and bake for 45–50 minutes, until golden brown and firm in the centre.
4. Leave to cool in the tin for 5 minutes, then loosen the edges with a palette knife and remove from the tin. Place on a wire rack to cool completely.
5. Slice into thin slices to serve.

MARY'S TIPS

Can be made up to a day before.

Freezes well.

Hot Puddings

Chocolate Steamed Pudding with Chocolate Sauce

Baked Boozy Peaches

Glazed Pineapple with Rum and Lime

Brioche Frangipane Apple Pudding

Pear and Blueberry Galette

Warm Chocolate Brownies

Classic Apple Cinnamon Crumble

Rhubarb Eve's Pudding

Classic Rice Pudding

Lemon Soufflé Pudding

Plum and Marzipan Tart

Chocolate Steamed Pudding with Chocolate Sauce

Rich and indulgent, this is such a comforting pudding. There's nothing tricky or clever, just a lovely light sponge that's rich in flavour and served with a divine pouring sauce.

Serves 6–8

125g (4½oz) baking spread straight from the fridge, plus extra for greasing
125g (4½oz) caster sugar
2 large eggs
100g (3½oz) self-raising flour
25g (1oz) cocoa powder, sifted

For the chocolate sauce
150ml (¼ pint) milk
150ml (¼ pint) pouring double cream
300g (10½oz) dark chocolate, broken into pieces

MARY'S TIPS

Can be made up to 4 hours ahead but don't turn it out – keep it warm in hot water. Sauce can be made up to a day ahead and reheated to serve.

Freezes well.

1. Grease a 1.1 litre (2 pint) pudding basin with baking spread, then cut a small square of non-stick baking paper (about the size of the base of the bowl), grease it and place in the base of the basin, pressing it into the corners.

2. Measure all the pudding ingredients into a mixing bowl. Whisk with an electric hand whisk until well blended, light and fluffy. Spoon the mixture into the basin and level the top.

3. Cut a square of foil about 4cm (1½in) bigger than the top rim of the pudding basin and grease the underside with baking spread. Make a pleat in the middle of the square. Place it on top of the basin and tightly press around the edges, then tie with string to seal.

4. Place a small plate or a trivet in the base of a deep saucepan. Place the basin on top and pour in enough boiling water to come halfway up the sides, then cover the pan with a lid. Bring the water back to the boil, then reduce the heat and simmer very gently for 1½–1¾ hours until firm to touch on top when gently pressed.

5. To make the chocolate sauce, measure the milk and cream into a saucepan. Heat until just boiling, then add the chocolate. Remove the pan from the heat and stir until the chocolate has melted.

6. Carefully remove the basin from the pan and remove the foil. To turn out, loosen around the edges with a knife, then turn upside down on to a plate and remove the bowl. Remove the paper on top. Pour some warm sauce over the pudding and cut into wedges to serve, with the remaining sauce in a jug.

Baked Boozy Peaches

Quick to make and beautifully warming, this recipe works well with nectarines, too. The marzipan caramelises and adds a delicious almond flavour, enhancing the natural sweetness of the peaches without being over-sweet, while the brandy and apple juice create a light sauce. It is best made and served straight away.

Serves 4–6

6 peaches (see tip)
8 tbsp brandy
4 tbsp apple juice or water
150g (5oz) golden marzipan, grated

1. Preheat the oven to 220°C/Fan 200°C/Gas 7.
2. Slice each peach in half and remove the stone. Place the peach halves cut-side up in an ovenproof dish that is wide enough to hold them in a single layer.
3. Mix the brandy with the apple juice or water and pour over the peaches. Pile some grated marzipan into the centre of each peach half, filling the hole where the stone used to be.
4. Bake in the oven for about 15 minutes, or until the marzipan is golden. Reduce the oven temperature to 180°C/Fan 160°C/Gas 4 and bake for a further 15 minutes, or until the peaches are soft and tender.
5. Serve warm with crème fraîche.

MARY'S TIPS

Try to buy peaches that are just under-ripe. If they're ripe, cook them for slightly less time on the second baking.

Not suitable for freezing.

Glazed Pineapple with Rum and Lime

Such a speedy, healthy pudding – perfect for camping or indeed any al fresco meal!

Serves 4

1 medium-sized ripe pineapple
3 tbsp light muscovado sugar
3 tbsp rum
Juice of ½ lime

1. Remove the base and top of the pineapple with a sharp knife and slice off the skin. Cut the pineapple lengthways into eight wedges, then remove and discard the core.
2. Heat a large griddle pan until very hot (see tip).
3. Mix the sugar and rum together in a small bowl. Brush the rum glaze all over the pineapple wedges, then place in the pan and chargrill for 1 minute on each side, or until golden and with griddle marks on the fruit.
4. Squeeze over the lime juice, drizzle with any extra rum syrup and serve straight away.

MARY'S TIPS

Make sure the pan is very hot – you just want to glaze the pineapple, not cook it, as it should still be firm when you eat it. Use a heavy-based frying pan if you don't have a griddle pan.

Best made and served immediately.

Not suitable for freezing.

Brioche Frangipane Apple Pudding

This tart uses really thin slices of brioche as a base, instead of pastry. They should be the thickness of pastry, though, so if you can only buy ready-sliced brioche, cut the slices horizontally to give 1cm (½in) pieces. When you feel in need of a comfort pudding, this one really fits the bill. It's perfect for Sunday lunch, served warm with ice cream, cream or crème fraîche.

Serves 8

- 8 × 1cm (½in) slices all-butter brioche loaf (about half a loaf)
- 175g (6oz) butter, softened, plus extra for greasing
- 175g (6oz) caster sugar
- 3 eggs, beaten
- 1 tsp almond extract
- 175g (6oz) ground almonds
- 25g (1oz) plain flour
- 2 large dessert apples, skin on, cored and thinly sliced
- 2 tbsp apricot jam
- 1 tbsp flaked almonds, toasted
- Icing sugar, for dusting

1. Preheat the oven to 200°C/Fan 180°C/Gas 6 and grease a large, shallow ovenproof dish, about 28cm (11in) diameter, with butter.

2. Arrange the brioche slices over the base of the dish. Make sure you cover the base and fill in all the gaps, but don't overlap the slices.

3. Measure the butter and sugar into a bowl and whiz until pale and fluffy with an electric hand whisk. Add the eggs and whiz again. Finally, add the almond extract, ground almonds and flour, then whiz until the mixture is soft and creamy and there are no lumps. Be careful not to over-process.

4. Spoon the mixture over the brioche base and spread it to the sides. Arrange the sliced apples in a neat overlapping circular pattern over the top. Bake the pudding in the preheated oven for about 40–50 minutes until lightly golden all over and firm in the centre when lightly pressed.

5. Meanwhile, melt the jam with 2 tablespoons of water in a small pan over a medium heat. Brush over the surface of the cooked pudding, then sprinkle with the flaked almonds. Dust the pudding with icing sugar and serve warm.

MARY'S TIPS

Can be made and baked up to a day ahead, and reheated to serve.

Freezes well. Defrost and reheat to serve.

Pear and Blueberry Galette

A comforting pudding that is so easy and quick to make. This would work well with tinned apricots or peaches as well. If you want to use fresh pears, peel and poach them until tender first.

Serves 8

- 75g (3oz) butter, softened, plus extra for greasing
- 75g (3oz) caster sugar
- 115g (4oz) self-raising flour
- 1 tsp baking powder
- 2 eggs
- 1 tsp vanilla extract
- 2 × 400g tins pear halves in natural juice
- 150g (5oz) fresh blueberries
- 2–3 tbsp redcurrant jelly, to glaze (optional)

1. Preheat the oven to 200°C/Fan 180°C/Gas 6. Grease a 28cm (11in) fluted loose-bottomed tin.
2. Measure the butter, sugar, flour, baking powder, eggs and vanilla into a bowl. Beat with an electric hand whisk until smooth. Spread the mixture to cover the base of the tin; it will make a very thin layer.
3. Drain the pear halves and cut each one lengthways into three long strips. Dry with kitchen paper. Arrange cut-side down over the surface of the batter in a neat pattern. Scatter the blueberries over the sponge in between the pears. Bake in the preheated oven for 20–25 minutes, until the sponge is lightly golden brown and well risen.
4. To glaze, if liked, melt the redcurrant jelly in a small saucepan over a low heat. Brush over the hot sponge and the fruit. Leave until just cool enough to handle, then remove from the tin and cut into wedges.
5. Serve warm with cream or crème fraîche.

MARY'S TIPS

Best made and served immediately. If you have some left over it reheats well.

Not suitable for freezing.

Warm Chocolate Brownies

The gooiest of brownies, moist and soft, and ideal as a decadent dessert to serve with ice cream. Wowee, delicious! These don't contain flour so are perfect for anyone who can't tolerate gluten.

Serves 8–10

350g (12oz) dark chocolate, broken into pieces
250g (9oz) butter, cubed, plus extra for greasing
300g (10½oz) dark muscovado sugar
6 eggs
75g (3oz) ground almonds

1. Preheat the oven to 180°C/Fan 160°C/Gas 4. Grease a 23 × 30cm (9 × 12in) traybake tin with butter and line with non-stick baking paper.

2. Place the chocolate and butter in a heatproof bowl. Set the bowl over a small saucepan of gently simmering water, making sure the bottom of the bowl does not touch the water. Heat through until runny and melted. Remove from the heat and set aside to cool slightly.

3. Measure the sugar into a separate bowl, add the eggs and whisk with an electric hand whisk until all the sugar has been incorporated. Carefully pour in the melted chocolate mixture and stir until evenly mixed. Fold in the ground almonds and gently stir to combine.

4. Pour into the prepared tin and bake in the oven for about 30 minutes, or until a light crust forms on top and the mixture is firm around the edges but still soft in the middle.

5. Leave to cool in the tin, to let the brownies set, then cut into squares (see tip) and serve with ice cream.

MARY'S TIPS

It's best to leave the cooked brownies in the tin, rather than trying to turn them over and peel off the baking paper. They are so gooey, the beautiful crust will be crushed if they are over-handled. Slice straight from the tin, and use a palette knife to remove each square.

Can be made up to a day ahead and reheated to serve warm. The cooked brownies freeze well.

Classic Apple Cinnamon Crumble

A classic crumble topping – no fancy oats or cereals, just full of flavour and perfect for a comforting pudding. Serve with custard, cream or ice cream.

Serves 6

25g (1oz) butter

1kg (2lb 4oz) cooking apples, peeled, cored and thickly sliced

75g (3oz) sultanas

1 tsp ground cinnamon

115g (4oz) demerara sugar

For the topping

175g (6oz) plain flour

75g (3oz) butter, cubed

55g (2oz) demerara sugar, plus 2 tbsp to sprinkle

25g (1oz) flaked almonds

1. You will need a shallow 1.5 litre (2½ pint) ovenproof dish. Preheat the oven to 200°C/Fan 180°C /Gas 6.
2. Melt the butter in a saucepan over a medium heat. Add the apples, sultanas, cinnamon and sugar, and stir over a high heat for 2–3 minutes until the sugar has melted. Spoon into the dish.
3. To make the crumble topping, measure the flour, butter and sugar into a bowl. Rub together using your fingertips until it resembles breadcrumbs, or add the ingredients to a food processor and whiz.
4. Sprinkle the crumble over the apples in the dish, then scatter over the flaked almonds and extra demerara sugar. Bake in the preheated oven for 45–50 minutes, or until lightly golden brown and bubbling.

MARY'S TIPS

The crumble can be assembled up to 6 hours ahead.

The uncooked crumble freezes well.

Rhubarb Eve's Pudding

A delicious alternative to the traditional Eve's pudding, this uses rhubarb instead of apples. Try to find young rhubarb, if you can, to give a lovely pink colour. Best made and served on the day, it would be great for Sunday lunch.

Serves 6

400g (14oz) young pink rhubarb
Finely grated zest and juice of 1 small orange
115g (4oz) demerara sugar
125g (4½oz) butter, softened
125g (4½oz) caster sugar
125g (4½oz) self-raising flour
1 tsp baking powder
2 eggs

1. You will need a 1.75 litre (3 pint) deep-sided ovenproof dish (about 20 x 25cm/8 x 10in – see tip). Preheat the oven to 180°C/Fan 160°C/Gas 4.
2. Remove any outer leaves or dry parts of the rhubarb stems, then cut into bite-sized pieces and tip into the baking dish. Pour over the orange juice. Sprinkle over half the demerara sugar and mix to combine. Make sure the rhubarb pieces are in a single layer.
3. To make the sponge, measure the butter, caster sugar, flour, baking powder and eggs into a bowl. Beat with a wooden spoon or an electric hand whisk until combined.
4. Stir in the orange zest, then spoon the batter over the rhubarb and sprinkle with the remaining demerara sugar. Bake in the preheated oven for 35–45 minutes, or until the sponge is golden brown, well risen and springy to the touch.
5. Serve warm with custard or cream.

MARY'S TIPS

The size of the dish matters for this recipe, because if it is too deep and narrow, the sponge will burn before the rhubarb is cooked. The fruit should lie in a single layer at the bottom.

Not suitable for freezing.

Classic Rice Pudding

Serve this with a bit of cream or a dollop of jam or syrup. Or just enjoy on its own – it's delicious as it is!

Serves 4–6

Butter, for greasing
115g (4oz) pudding rice
900ml (1½ pints) full-fat milk (see tip)
55g (2oz) caster sugar
½ tsp freshly grated nutmeg (optional)

1. Preheat the oven to 160°C/Fan 140°C/Gas 3 and well grease a 1.6 litre (2¾ pint) wide-based ovenproof dish with butter.
2. Tip the rice into the dish. Heat the milk in a saucepan (see tip) and pour over the rice, then add the sugar and stir to combine.
3. Bake in the oven for about 30 minutes. Stir gently and sprinkle with a dusting of nutmeg, if using. Continue cooking for a further 1¼–1½ hours, until a golden skin has formed on top and the rice is soft and tender underneath.
4. Serve hot with jam or syrup.

MARY'S TIPS

Full-fat milk gives the best rich flavour, though semi-skimmed would be fine too. If you only have semi-skimmed, add a little less and make up the full amount with cream.

Heating the milk gets the cooking going.

Not suitable for freezing.

Lemon Soufflé Pudding

This is one of my most favourite hot puddings.

Serves 6

115g (4oz) butter, softened, plus extra for greasing

175g (6oz) caster sugar

Finely grated zest and juice of 3 lemons

4 large eggs, separated

75g (3oz) plain flour

450ml (¾ pint) full-fat milk

1. Preheat the oven to 180°C/Fan 160°C/Gas 4 and grease a 1.8 litre (3¼ pint) wide-based, shallow ovenproof dish with butter.

2. Measure the butter and sugar into a bowl and whisk with an electric hand whisk until pale and creamy. Add the lemon zest and juice and whisk again until combined. Whisk in the egg yolks and half the flour. Add the remaining flour, wiping down the sides of the bowl with a spatula to incorporate every last bit of mixture. Pour in the milk, a little at a time, and whisk until the mix looks slightly curdled.

3. In a separate bowl, whisk the egg whites until they look like a cloud (see tip). Add 1 heaped tablespoon of the egg whites to the batter and mix well. Fold the remaining whites into the batter, until you have a smooth mixture.

4. Gently pour the batter into the prepared dish (see tip), then place the dish in a large, high-sided roasting tin and fill with enough boiling water to come halfway up the sides of the dish. Carefully place in the oven and bake for 30–35 minutes, until lightly golden and well risen, with a slight wobble in the centre. Serve at once.

MARY'S TIPS

Don't forget to wash the beaters of the electric whisk before whisking the egg whites. Like the mixing bowl, they must be clean and completely grease-free or the whites will not whip.

When the batter is made, it is important to pour it into the ovenproof dish carefully to make sure that none of the air is knocked out. Lift the dish gently, trying not to knock or bang it down.

Not suitable for freezing.

Plum and Marzipan Tart

A wonderful pudding to make when plums are in season. The marzipan gives great flavour and prevents the pastry from going soggy.

Serves 6

8 ripe plums, destoned and quartered
25g (1oz) light muscovado sugar
2 tbsp cornflour
1 × 500g block puff pastry
100g (3½oz) golden marzipan, grated
1 egg, beaten
2 tbsp demerara sugar
Icing sugar, to decorate

1. Preheat the oven to 200°C/Fan 180°C/Gas 6 and place a flat baking tray in the oven to get hot.
2. Tip the plum quarters into a bowl. Add the muscovado sugar and cornflour and mix well. Leave to stand for 10 minutes so the juices release from the plums. Mix again so the plums are well coated.
3. Place the pastry on a lightly floured work surface. Roll out the pastry to a circle and trim to about 33cm (13in) in diameter. Transfer the pastry to a piece of non-stick baking paper and prick all over with a fork. Scatter the marzipan over the middle of the pastry.
4. Tip the plum mixture over the marzipan and spread out slightly, leaving a 3cm (1¼in) border. Brush the bare pastry edges with the beaten egg, then fold and twist the pastry over, and push together to make sides (a bit like the edge of a Cornish pasty). Brush the edges with more egg, then sprinkle with the demerara sugar.
5. Lift the paper and tart onto the hot baking tray, then return to the preheated oven for about 35–40 minutes until golden and crisp.
6. Sprinkle with icing sugar to serve.

MARY'S TIPS

Best made and served immediately. If you have some left over it reheats well.

Not suitable for freezing.

Cold Desserts

Quickest-ever Lemon Meringue Pie

Lemon Ripple Ice Cream

Velvet Chocolate Torte

Scots Whisky Cream

Almond Meringue Roulade

Strawberry and White Chocolate Cheesecake

Mango Passion

Summer Days Pavlova

Sunrise Fruit Salad

Cheat's Apricot Trifle

Quickest-ever Lemon Meringue Pie

This is a cheat's recipe! With no pastry and no long, complicated method for making the lemon filling, it is straightforward to prepare, and a lovely variation on the classic dish. The first piece will be difficult to get out, as we cook it in a dish that you can take to the table, rather than a tin, but after that it's simple.

Serves 6

For the base

100g (3½oz) butter

175g (6oz) digestive biscuits, finely crushed (see tip)

For the filling

1 × 397g tin full-fat sweetened condensed milk (see tip)

3 egg yolks

Finely grated zest and juice of 2 large lemons

For the topping

3 egg whites

175g (6oz) caster sugar

MARY'S TIPS

To crush the biscuits, place in a plastic bag, seal shut and use a rolling pin to bash to a fine crumb.

Make sure you use full-fat condensed milk, or the filling will not set.

Not suitable for freezing.

1. You will need a 24cm (9½in) round straight-sided or fluted dish, about 4cm (1½in) deep. Preheat the oven to 180°C/Fan 160°C/Gas 4.

2. Melt the butter in a medium saucepan, remove the pan from the heat and stir in the biscuit crumbs. Press the mixture into the bottom of the dish with the back of a spoon, bringing the crumbs up the sides of the dish, and smooth the base in an even layer.

3. To make the filling, first pour the condensed milk into a bowl. Beat in the egg yolks, lemon zest and strained juice. The mixture will appear to thicken on standing, then loosen again as soon as it is stirred. This is caused by the combination of condensed milk and lemon juice and is nothing to worry about. Pour the mixture into the biscuit-lined dish.

4. Put the egg whites into a large, clean, grease-free bowl and whisk with an electric hand whisk until they look like clouds. Start adding the caster sugar, a teaspoon at a time, whisking between each addition, with the electric hand whisk on full speed.

5. Spoon the meringue over the surface of the filling, then spread gently with the back of a spoon to cover the filling up to the biscuit-lined edges. Lightly swirl the surface of the meringue, then bake for 30 minutes, or until the meringue is pale golden. Set aside for about 30 minutes to allow the filling to firm up, before serving warm.

Lemon Ripple Ice Cream

Ice cream is always a comfort food, whether on its own in the summer to refresh you on a warm day or served with a delicious dessert in winter. This recipe is so simple to make – no special ice cream machine needed.

Serves 6

4 eggs, separated
115g (4oz) caster sugar
300ml (½ pint) pouring double cream
Finely grated zest of 2 lemons
1 x 300–325g jar luxury lemon curd

1. Place the egg whites in a large mixing bowl. Using an electric hand whisk, whisk on full speed until the whites look like a cloud. Gradually add the sugar, whisking on maximum speed, until you have a thick, glossy meringue.
2. In a separate bowl, beat the egg yolks with a fork. Add them to the meringue mixture and stir until smooth.
3. In a separate bowl, whisk the cream into soft peaks using an electric hand whisk. Add the cream to the meringue with the lemon zest and half the curd. Gently fold everything together until smooth.
4. Spoon the mixture into a shallow container. Blob the remaining curd on top and swirl into the mixture to make a ripple effect. Freeze for at least 12 hours before serving.

MARY'S TIP

Freezes well for up to 3 months.

Velvet Chocolate Torte

Yes, it really does serve 12, it is so rich! If you do not have a springform tin, spoon the mixture into a freezer-safe bowl, cover with clingfilm, then freeze. After defrosting for 20 minutes, the torte will be ready to spoon on to serving plates and be decorated with strawberries.

Serves 12

200g (7oz) dark chocolate, broken into pieces
115g (4oz) caster sugar
6 tbsp water
4 egg yolks
2 tbsp brandy
600ml (1pint) pouring double cream

To serve

12 large strawberries, hulled and sliced
A little single cream

MARY'S TIPS

The torte can be frozen in the tin for up to 3 days. For longer freezing, once the torte is firmly frozen, remove it from the tin, wrap in more clingfilm and seal in a plastic bag. Freeze for up to 3 months.

1. Oil a 20cm (8in) loose-bottomed or springform tin and line with clingfilm.
2. Place the chocolate in a food processor and process for 1 minute, or until just a few pieces remain in the otherwise powdery chocolate. Alternatively, finely grate the chocolate.
3. Measure the sugar and water into a small pan and place over a low heat until the sugar has dissolved, stirring occasionally. Turn up the heat and boil for 3–4 minutes, until a thin syrup.
4. Set the processor running and pour the hot syrup through the funnel on to the chocolate so it melts. Add just a little boiling water if some unmelted chocolate remains.
5. Add the egg yolks to the chocolate and process for a few seconds before adding the brandy. If you are not using a processor, beat the ingredients with an electric hand whisk.
6. In a separate bowl, whisk the cream to a soft, floppy consistency, then fold in the chocolate mixture. Spread into the prepared tin, levelling the surface. Cover with clingfilm and transfer to the freezer for a minimum of 6 hours.
7. Take the torte from the freezer 20 minutes before serving. Remove from the tin, strip away the clingfilm, and put on a plate to defrost; it should still be slightly frozen when it is cut.
8. Place a wedge of chocolate torte in the centre of a plate and arrange strawberry slices around each serving. Drizzle a little cream over each portion, if liked, and serve immediately.

Scots Whisky Cream

Quick and delicious, this dish reminds me of wonderful holidays taken in Scotland over the years. Putting pared rind into the syrup while it's cooking, and then removing it once the syrup has cooled, allows the lovely orange flavour to infuse the syrup without affecting the texture of the finished cream. It's quite rich, so serve in small shot glasses or little pots.

Serves 8–10

100ml (3½fl oz) whisky
115g (4oz) caster sugar
3 tbsp fine-cut orange marmalade
Juice of ½ orange
Pared rind of ½ orange (see tip)
450ml (¾ pint) pouring double cream
24–30 fresh raspberries, to decorate

1. Measure the whisky, sugar and marmalade into a small saucepan. Add the orange juice and pared rind. Stir over a medium heat until the sugar has dissolved and the marmalade has melted (see tip). Bring to the boil, then allow to bubble for a minute. Remove from the heat and leave to cool in the pan for an hour.

2. Remove the orange rind from the syrup and set aside. Pour the syrup into a large bowl. Add the cream and whisk, using an electric hand whisk, until soft peaks form.

3. Spoon into 8 or 10 clear shot glasses or cups, and top each portion with 2 or 3 raspberries and a few strips of the reserved orange rind. Keep chilled in the fridge until ready to serve.

MARY'S TIPS

The easiest way to pare the rind is with a vegetable peeler – take off the skin but as little pith as possible, which would make the flavour bitter, and then cut into fine strips.

When heating the syrup, make sure the sugar has completely dissolved before letting the mixture boil, or the syrup will be grainy. If it starts to bubble before the marmalade and sugar have dissolved, turn the heat down and proceed on a gentle heat until ready to boil.

Can be made up to 4 hours ahead and kept in the fridge.

Not suitable for freezing.

Almond Meringue Roulade

A meringue roulade may seem tricky to make, but it is fairly straightforward if you read the recipe carefully!

Serves 8–10

Butter, for greasing
5 egg whites
275g (10oz) caster sugar
55g (2oz) flaked almonds
300ml (½ pint) pouring double cream
2 tbsp Baileys cream liqueur or brandy
225g (8oz) fresh raspberries

MARY'S TIPS

Best made on the day it is served.

Freezes well rolled but the surface does not remain crisp.

1. Preheat the oven to 200°C/Fan 180°C/Gas 6. Line a 33 × 23cm (13 × 9in) Swiss roll tin with greased non-stick baking paper.
2. Whisk the egg whites in bowl with an electric hand whisk, or in a mixer on full speed, until very stiff. Gradually add the sugar, a heaped teaspoon at a time, whisking at high speed all the time. Whisk until very, very stiff and glossy, and all the sugar has been included.
3. Spread onto the prepared tin and sprinkle the almonds evenly over the top. Bake in the oven for about 12 minutes or until pale cream in colour.
4. Lower the oven temperature to 160°C/Fan 140°C /Gas 3 and continue to bake for a further 20 minutes until firm to the touch.
5. Remove the meringue from the oven and leave to cool for a few minutes. Turn it out on to a sheet of non-stick baking paper, almond-side down. Remove the paper from the base of the meringue and leave to cool completely.
6. Whip the cream in a large bowl to soft peaks, then stir in the Baileys or brandy. Fold in the raspberries. Spread the raspberry cream over the meringue to the edges. Starting to roll from one long end, roll the meringue tightly like a Swiss roll. Wrap the rolled meringue in non-stick baking paper and chill in the fridge.
7. Transfer to a large serving plate and gently remove the baking paper to serve.

Strawberry and White Chocolate Cheesecake

The surface of the baked cheesecake may crack slightly in the middle, but don't worry – this is part of its charm! To avoid a really deep crack, loosen the tin around the edge before the cheesecake becomes cold. You can make this the night before, and it freezes well, wrapped, once it's cooled.

Serves 8–10

For the base

55g (2oz) butter
150g (5oz) plain chocolate digestive biscuits, crushed

For the filling

300g (10½oz) good-quality white chocolate, broken into pieces
400g (14oz) full-fat cream cheese
2 eggs
150ml (¼ pint) soured cream
1 tsp vanilla extract
400g (14oz) fresh strawberries, hulled and thickly sliced
4 tbsp strawberry jam

1. Preheat the oven to 160°C/Fan 140°C/Gas 3. Grease the base of a 20cm (8in) deep springform cake tin with oil and line with a circle of non-stick baking paper.

2. Melt the butter in a small saucepan over a low heat. Stir in the crushed biscuits to coat. Press evenly into the base of the prepared tin. Chill in the fridge.

3. Place the white chocolate in a heatproof bowl and sit over a pan of simmering water (do not allow the chocolate to become too hot), stirring occasionally with a spoon until runny and smooth.

4. Whisk the cream cheese and eggs together in a large bowl with an electric hand whisk until smooth. Add the soured cream and vanilla and whisk again until completely smooth with no lumps. Stir in the melted chocolate and mix together.

5. Pour the white chocolate mixture into the tin over the biscuit base and spread evenly. Bake in the preheated oven for about 45 minutes, or until firm around the edge and just set in the middle. Remove from the oven and run a small palette knife around the edge of the tin. Set aside to cool, and then chill.

6. When ready to serve, remove the outside ring and lift the base on to a serving plate. Arrange the strawberries in a neat pattern to give a spiral effect on top of the cheesecake. Warm the jam in a small pan over a gentle heat to loosen, then pour through a sieve into a bowl. Using a brush, use the jam to glaze the strawberries.

MARY'S TIPS

Best made on the day it is served.

Freezes well without the decoration.

Mango Passion

Very easy to make, this dessert is better when made ahead as it allows the flavours of the mango and passion fruit to develop in the cream and yoghurt, and the dark sugar topping has time to liquify and sweeten each spoonful as you eat. Delicious – this is one of Lucy's favourite flavour combinations.

Serves 6

1 large ripe mango
3 ripe passion fruit
500g (1lb 2oz) full-fat Greek yoghurt
150ml (¼ pint) pouring double cream, lightly whipped
6 tbsp light muscovado sugar

1. You will need 6 stemmed glasses or syllabub cups.
2. Slice the flesh from each side of the flat mango stone. Remove the peel and cut the flesh in cubes. Try to remove as much flesh as possible from around the stone, then peel and cube this too.
3. Using a teaspoon, scoop the seeds and flesh from the passion fruit into a bowl then mix with the yoghurt and cream.
4. Put an equal quantity of the mango in each glass then fill with the yoghurt mixture. Chill for up to 8 hours.
5. An hour or so before serving, remove the glasses from the fridge and sprinkle a tablespoon of the sugar over each one. Return to the fridge until ready to serve.

MARY'S TIPS

These will keep in the fridge for up to XX hours.

Not suitable for freezing.

Summer Days Pavlova

Wonderfully impressive pavlova, bursting with colour and flavour.

Serves 8–10

5 egg whites
300g (10½oz) caster sugar
2 tsp white wine vinegar
2 tsp cornflour
400ml (14fl oz) pouring double cream
4 heaped tbsp Greek yoghurt
400g (14oz) strawberries, hulled and sliced into quarters

For the coulis

300g (10½oz) fresh raspberries
1 heaped tbsp

MARY'S TIPS

Best made to serve.

Not suitable for freezing.

1. Preheat the oven to 160°C/Fan 140°C/Gas 3. Lay a piece of non-stick baking paper on a baking tray and draw a 25cm (10in) circle on it.

2. Tip the egg whites into a large bowl and whisk with an electric hand whisk or in a free-standing mixer on the fastest speed until stiff. While still whisking on maximum speed, gradually add generous teaspoons of caster sugar, until the mixture is stiff and shiny and stands in peaks.

3. In a cup, blend the vinegar and cornflour together and mix until smooth. Stir this into the meringue mixture.

4. Spread two-thirds of the meringue mixture onto the paper to give a 25cm/10in circle. Fill a piping bag with the remaining meringue and fit with a rose nozzle. Carefully pipe about 8 separate little nests positioned equally around the edge of the circle. Slide the meringue into the middle of the preheated oven and immediately turn the heat down to 150°C/Fan 130°C/Gas 2. Bake for 1 hour, then turn the oven off and leave the meringue in the oven to become cold, or until it easily comes off the paper.

5. Meanwhile, to make the coulis, tip half the raspberries and the icing sugar into a food processor and whiz until smooth. Pass through a sieve to remove the seeds.

6. In a large bowl, whip the cream to soft peaks, then fold in the Greek yoghurt.

7. Spoon some cream mixture into each of the nests, then tip the remaining mixture into the centre. Swirl a little coulis into each pile of cream, then scatter the remaining raspberries and strawberries over the top. Serve with the remaining coulis alongside.

Sunrise Fruit Salad

Fresh, wonderful colour and ideal for a dessert or breakfast with Greek yoghurt.

Serves 4–6

- 1 ripe mango, peeled and sliced into thin strips
- 1 small cantaloupe melon, peeled and cut into cubes
- 1 small ripe papaya, peeled, deseeded and cut into thin, short matchsticks
- 3 ripe passion fruit, halved
- 100ml (3½fl oz) orange juice, from a carton
- Seeds from 1 pomegranate

1. Place the mango, melon and papaya in a large bowl.
2. Scoop out the seeds and juice from the passion fruit and stir into the fruits. Pour in the orange juice and place in the fridge to chill.
3. Scatter with pomegranate seeds before serving chilled.

MARY'S TIPS

Can be assembled up to 6 hours ahead.

Not suitable for freezing.

Cheat's Apricot Trifle

No Christmas table is complete without a trifle – this one's a cheat because I use shop-bought custard and sponges. The trifle benefits from being made in advance as the flavours have a chance to mingle and develop. If you don't have a large trifle bowl, this could be made easily in 12 individual wine glasses, or other pretty glasses.

Serves 8

12 trifle sponges (250g/9oz in total)
½ jar apricot jam
2 × 410g tins apricot halves in light syrup
6 tbsp brandy
1 × 400g tin custard
2 tsp vanilla extract
600ml (1 pint) pouring double cream
30g (1oz) flaked almonds, toasted

1. You will need a 2.5 litre (4½ pint) glass trifle dish with a wide 25cm (10in) base (see tip).
2. Slice each trifle sponge in half horizontally. Spread the apricot jam over one half of each slice and sandwich together with the other half.
3. Drain the apricots, reserving 100ml (3½fl oz) syrup from the tin. Add the brandy to the reserved syrup, and chop the apricot halves into pieces.
4. Arrange the sandwiched trifle sponges in the base of the glass trifle bowl. Cut and press them to make sure all the pieces fit. Pour over the brandy and apricot syrup, then press the sponges again, so they are soaked in the liquid.
5. Pour the custard into a bowl and stir in the vanilla. Whip 150ml (¼ pint) of the cream and stir it into the custard. Spoon this mixture over the apricots, level the surface and transfer to the fridge for 1 hour or overnight.
6. Whip the remaining cream to soft peaks, then spread or pipe the cream over the top of the custard on the day of serving. Scatter with the toasted flaked almonds to serve.

MARY'S TIPS

It is important to use a wide dish. A narrow, taller bowl will make the sponge base too thick.

This can be made a day ahead and kept, covered, in the fridge. The final layer of cream and the almonds should be added no more than a few hours before serving.

Not suitable for freezing.

Weights

Metric	Imperial
5g	⅛oz
10g	¼oz
15g	½oz
20g	¾oz
25/30g	1oz
35g	1¼oz
40g	1½oz
55g	2oz
65g	2½oz
75g	3oz
80g	3¼oz
100g	3½oz
115g	4oz
125g	4½oz
150g	5oz
165g	5½oz
175g	6oz
200g	7oz
225g	8oz
250g	9oz
275g	10oz
300g	10½oz
325g	11½oz
350g	12oz
360g	12½oz
375g	13oz
400g	14oz
425g	15oz
450g	1lb
500g	1lb 2oz
525g	1lb 3oz
550g	1¼lb

Metric	Imperial
600g	1lb 5oz
650g	1lb 7oz
675g	1½lb
700g	1lb 9oz
750g	1lb 10oz
800g	1¾lb
850g	1lb 14oz
900g	2lb
1kg	2lb 4oz
1.25kg	2lb 12oz
1.3kg	3lb
1.5kg	3lb 5oz
1.7kg	3lb 12oz
1.8kg	4lb
2kg	4lb 7oz
2.25kg	5lb

Oven Temperatures

°C	Fan °C	°F	Gas Mark
120	100	250	½
140	120	275	1
150	130	300	2
160	140	325	3
180	160	350	4
190	170	375	5
200	180	400	6
220	200	425	7
230	210	450	8
240	220	475	9

Volume

Metric	Imperial
30ml	1fl oz
50ml	2fl oz
75ml	2½ fl oz
85ml	3fl oz
100ml	3½fl oz
125ml	4fl oz
150ml	5fl oz (¼ pint)
175ml	6fl oz
200ml	7fl oz (⅓ pint)
225ml	8fl oz
240ml	8½fl oz
250ml	9fl oz
275ml	9½fl oz
300ml	10fl oz (½ pint)
350ml	12fl oz
400ml	14fl oz
450ml	15fl oz (¾ pint)
500ml	18fl oz
600ml	20fl oz (1 pint)
750ml	1¼ pints
900ml	1½ pints
1 litre	1¾ pints
1.2 litres	2 pints
1.5 litres	2½ pints
1.75 litres	3 pints
2 litres	3½ pints
2.25 litres	4 pints
2.5 litres	4½ pints
2.75 litres	5 pints
3.4 litres	6 pints
3.9 litres	7 pints
4.5 litres	8 pints (1 gallon)

Measurements

Metric	Imperial
5mm	¼in
1cm	½in
1.5cm	⅝in
2cm	¾in
2.5cm	1in
3cm	1¼in
4cm	1½in
5cm	2in
6cm	2¼in
6.5cm	2½in
7cm	2¾in
7.5cm	3in
9cm	3½in
10cm	4in
11cm	4½in
12.5cm	5in
15cm	6in
16cm	6½in
18cm	7in
20cm	8in
23cm	9in
25cm	10in
28cm	11in
30cm	12in
33cm	13in
35cm	13¾in
36cm	14in
40cm	15¼in
46cm	18in

Index

A

B

C

D

E

F

G

H

I

J

L

M

R

S

SO MANY THANK YOUS

Firstly, thank you to Lucy Young, 36 years by my side – thinking the same and together we have the same high standards. She runs the show and my working life. She is brilliant and always so loyal, and for that I am so grateful.

Lucinda McCord, Thursdays are special days when she arrives early and we set to testing new recipes and ideas. Luce, Lucinda and I, with notebooks in hand, make and taste until the recipes are perfect. Lucinda has perfect attention to detail and speed; she truly is the best.

To BBC Books, led by Albert De Petrillo, Publishing Director, such a pleasure to work with you. We love our meetings and thank you to Phoebe Lindsley, Commissioning Editor, who brings the creativity, and to the uncompromising Jo Roberts-Miller our editor who we have worked with for over 20 years. Thanks also to designer Abi Hartshorne.

For the photoshoots, I'd like to thank the exceptional Lisa Harrison, home economist, assisted by Alice Hughes, for the props, the effervescent Sophie Robinson, and for the stunning photography, Tara Fisher, this is our third book with Tara, all shot in her studio in London. Thank you to you all.

To the glam squad, Jo Penford, for hair and make up and general joy, for styling, Tess Wright, who always finds that perfect outfit for the cover shoot. Huge thanks to photographer Nicky Johnson for the cover pics - portraits are Nicky's forte and he is the very best and brings the laughter too.

Caroline Wood, our literary agent, how lucky we are to be guided by you, supported by Michele Topham, who has worked with us for more years than I can remember. Thank you to you both.

Thank you to you all and to our readers for everlasting support.

Love Mary

BBC Books

UK | USA | Canada | Ireland | Australia
India | New Zealand | South Africa

BBC Books is part of the Penguin Random House group of companies whose addresses can be found at global.penguinrandomhouse.com

Penguin Random House UK
One Embassy Gardens, 8 Viaduct Gardens, London SW11 7BW

penguin.co.uk
global.penguinrandomhouse.com

Penguin Random House UK

First published by BBC Books in 2026

1

Food Photography by Tara Fisher
Photography of Mary Berry by Nicky Johnston

Publishing Director: Albert DePetrillo
Project Editor and Copyeditor: Jo Roberts-Miller
Commissioning Editor: Phoebe Lindsley
Editorial Assistant: Clementine Lussiana
Production Controller: Antony Heller
Designer: Hart Studio
Food Stylist: Lisa Harrison
Assistant Food Stylist: Alice Hughes
Prop Stylist: Sophie Louise Robinson

Colour origination by Altaimage Ltd
Printed and bound in Germany by Mohn Media Mohndruck GmbH

The authorised representative in the EEA is Penguin Random House Ireland, Morrison Chambers, 32 Nassau Street, Dublin D02 YH68.

A CIP catalogue record for this book is available from the British Library

ISBN 9781785949890

Penguin Random House is committed to a sustainable future for our business, our readers and our planet. This book is made from Forest Stewardship Council® certified paper.

FSC www.fsc.org MIX Paper FSC™ C018179